BEYOND
THE VALLEY

finding hope in life's losses

BEYOND THE VALLEY

DAVE BRANON

DISCOVERY HOUSE
PUBLISHERS®

Discovery House Publishers is affiliated with RBC Ministries, Grand Rapids, Michigan.

Requests for permission to quote from this book should be directed to: Permissions Department, Discovery House Publishers, P.O. Box 3566, Grand Rapids, MI 49501 or contact us by e-mail at permissionsdept@dhp.org

"I Still Believe" by Jeremy Camp, copyright © 2002 Stolen Pride Music (ASCAP) Thirsty Moon River Publ. Inc. (ASCAP) (adm. by EMI CMG Publishing). International copyright secured. All rights reserved. Used by permission.

Scripture taken from the HOLY BIBLE, NEW INTERNATIONAL VERSION®, NIV®. Copyright ©1973, 1978, 1984 by Biblica, Inc.™ Used by permission of Zondervan. All rights reserved worldwide. www.zondervan.com

Interior design by Melissa Elenbaas

Library of Congress Cataloging-in-Publication Data

Branon, Dave.
Beyond the valley : finding hope in life's losses / Dave Branon.
　　p. cm.
ISBN 978-1-57293-373-6
　　1. Loss (Psychology)--Religious aspects--Christianity. 2. Consolation. I. Title.
BV4905.3.B73 2010
248.8'6--dc22　　　　　　　　　　　　　　　　　2010010930

Printed in the United States of America
Third printing in 2012

CONTENTS

INTRODUCTION

I never planned to have valleys on the topographical map of my life. My map, as I saw it, would always consist of the high road. The smooth road. The pathway lit up by God's love and decorated with His gift of the abundant life. It was to be the journey of the trying-to-be-godly-but-appreciating-a-forgiving-God Christian. The walk of the trusting believer.

Yet here I am, still surprised and shocked to be walking through the valley of the shadow of death.

The way I figured it, my wife and I would raise up our four kids in the way they should go, and when we were old they would all be there to take care of us.

We were thirty years into this marriage-and-family thing, and we were enjoying God's continued blessing.

We loved the stuffing out of life. Not that every day was always easy and full of smiles and laughing, but for the most part, our direction was still heading securely toward the road to blessedness. Up on the mountain. Far from the valley.

Take Thursday, June 6, 2002, for instance.

It was a typical day in the light of God's grace. In fact, it was a bright, sunny, warm day that reminded us that the good times of summer were about to shine across our lives. And since it was the last day of school, our kids were enjoying the lightheartedness of impending vacation.

At home on that evening, my fifteen-year-old son Steve and I had settled in to keep an eye on the Detroit Red Wings' hockey game. We weren't huge hockey fans, but this was the Stanley Cup playoffs and these were our Red Wings, so we were tuned in.

Julie, our second-oldest daughter, had just come home from her summer job at a grocery store, reminding us again that this job made her extremely thankful that she had just graduated from college and would soon be heading for her first teaching job at a Christian school in Florida.

Indeed, the sisters—Julie, Lisa (our oldest, who lived in Ohio with her husband Todd and was a schoolteacher), and our youngest daughter, Melissa—had already purchased plane tickets for an all-sisters vacation in Orlando, Florida. The sisters (born strategically four years apart, each in July) were to take in the wonderful world of Disney, and then the rest of us would show up at Pompano Beach to move Julie and her stuff into her place near the Christian school where she would be debuting as a teacher.

The summer looked bright enough to call for sunglasses.

But back to our June 6 evening. Sue, my wife, was reading the paper, winding down her day and preparing to go to bed. She had to be on the job early the next day at the nursing home where she was a nurse—and where Melissa worked part-time. Mell, too, would be working on Friday.

Sue didn't want to go to bed until she knew Melissa was safely home. Mell was at a cottage on Lake Michigan with some school friends where the parents hosted an end-of-school party of pizza, jet-skiing, and just good times. Melissa had called her mom at eight o'clock to tell us she would be on her way home with her boyfriend Jordan at nine.

The path of our life had been so direct. Four kids. Four kids who had trusted Jesus and made us proud. The pathway of a family with its eye on loving each other and honoring God in life. We could see the valley, but it seemed so far away as to be inaccessible.

Yet at just after nine p.m. on that gorgeous Michigan spring night, our lives veered off the path we thought would be ours for the rest of our time on earth. We careened off that pathway and went straight into the valley—an unfamiliar, dark, and deep ravine of near hopelessness.

While Jordan and Melissa were on their way home that evening, traveling on an unfamiliar road, Jordan pulled his car into an intersection—where it was hit broadside by another teen driver.

Melissa, our seventeen-year-old daughter and sister—a girl who loved to cook odd concoctions in the kitchen, who never liked to be idle for a minute, who played varsity softball and volleyball, who had a solid though not flashy faith in Jesus, who was a bright light of joy and love to her many friends at school and church, and who had grown from a frightened little preschooler into a self-confident teen—was killed instantly.

Our family was plunged into a new existence. Now the mountaintop was so far away we couldn't see it.

Suddenly, and without warning, we found ourselves walking numbly through the valley of the shadow of death. We were thrust into the place where we had to test the Psalm 23 promise that God's presence will make sure we "fear no evil."

We found ourselves in a far different place than we had ever been in before.

A place where life is not as much fun as it used to be.

A place where harmless words from well-meaning others can turn into unshakeable irritants.

A place where hearing other people harmlessly laughing often seems completely incongruous with how we feel.

A place where the God we knew and loved and served sometimes seems more mysterious than knowable—and we realized this just at the time we needed Him the most, when we first arrived in the valley.

Have you ever been in the valley? The valley that comes with life's troubles and pain?

If so, or if you have ever walked with those who dwell in its misty atmosphere, I invite you to walk along with me for a while. As I journey, I am continually seeking the help of the One who promised never to leave me. I'm begging the One who said not to fear to give me peace. I'm pleading with the God of all comfort to explain what that word means to the uncomfortable. I'm clinging with all my might to the One who said I could never be plucked from His hand. I'm struggling to trust completely the One I trusted with my daughter—knowing that she now dwells in His presence and not mine.

Walk with me, won't you? Together, we can find hope, solace, comfort, and sometimes even joy—while seeking to go beyond the valley.

CHAPTER
ONE

THE LORD, MY SHEPHERD

We all need a shepherd—a guide, a protector. Both in life's easy times and in its moments of pain, we can turn to One who knows trouble, who knows the future, and who knows how to comfort us the best when we need it the most.

THE GOD FATHER

What's behind it . . .

I can't seem to figure God out.

That's a good thing.

It's good because God is so much greater than we are that it would be foolish to suggest that we've got the God-thing down pat.

A lot of people in our world can't figure God out, so they choose not to worship Him. They say they can't understand how God and poverty can co-exist because, in their finite way of thinking, God should simply eliminate economic difficulty.

But not figuring God out is a good thing because it reminds us that He is so much greater and more complicated and more nuanced than we could ever understand.

And not figuring God out leads us to a couple of other positive results:

First, it allows us to exercise our faith. When things go wrong and God doesn't write the reasons across the sky, we are left with the good option of simply trusting that He knows what He is doing.

And second, not figuring God out completely leads us to spend time contemplating Him and sitting in awe of Him. Somewhat like we do when we see great art and have to spend time puzzling it all out, we sit enthralled at our majestic God. We read passages like 2 Corinthians 1:3, and we have the joy of piecing together what it means to us.

Walk with me through this verse and see how exciting it is to contemplate our awesome heavenly Father.

GOD'S WORD ON IT . . .

Praise be to the God and Father of our Lord Jesus Christ, the Father of compassion and the God of all comfort.
2 Corinthians 1:3

SERIOUS CONTEMPLATION . . .

Praise escapes our lips most easily during the good times in our lives.

We love to grace the Sunday morning scene with flowing words of honor and worship as a comfortable congregation joins in a chorus of music and praise singing.

We cherish the chance to speak great words of reverence to our God when our prayers come back marked "Answered!"

"Praise be!" says Paul as he begins his letter—and we value his example and our great opportunity to echo his words.

As we examine the object of the praise Paul tells us about in this passage, though, we can see a progression away from a life free of problems and toward one of struggles—a life that—regardless of our feelings—should still be marked by the same kind of praise we offered when we stood atop life's mountain peaks.

Paul offers praise first to the "God . . . of our Lord Jesus Christ." That single idea fills us with both wonder and mystery as we marvel in the truth of God's triune nature. While we know in our heart and in our biblically educated minds that God exists in three persons—Father, Son, and Spirit—we stand amazed that God the Father is not just our God, but He is also the God of our Lord Jesus Christ.

We are able to praise the God who co-existed with Jesus from eternity past yet superintended His sacrificial death for us on the cross. We send glory God's way because when Jesus said, "It is finished," God's work of appropriating salvation for all who believe in Jesus was being fulfilled.

Indeed, we "praise the God of our Lord Jesus Christ!"

Paul's next offering of praise goes to God in a little different way. "Praise be to the . . . Father of our Lord Jesus

Christ." We sense something different—something more familial and warm this time as Paul expresses glory to God's role as the Father in the triune Godhead.

The heavenly Father. The One who first loved us. The One who is "in heaven" and possesses the hallowed name. The One whom Jesus asked to forgive the ones who didn't know what they were doing when they killed Him. The One who loved the "Son and placed everything in His hands."

Indeed, we "praise the Father of our Lord Jesus Christ."

Paul goes on—and here those of us who have stubbed our toes on the rocks of life's difficulties get some valued help.

The apostle sends praise next to the "Father of compassion." Here is where those of us who have fallen off the mountain of life and are making our way through one of the valleys of trouble find the strength to stop and shout praise. Yes, we need to praise the God of our Lord and the Father of our Lord—but our hearts covet compassion.

Struggles may threaten to surround us like a rain-swollen river that has breached its banks, and we need Somebody who cares. We need compassion. And Paul points us to that One.

The Father of compassion is "father to the fatherless, a defender of widows" (Psalm 68:5), never leaving the seemingly helpless without resource.

The Father of compassion is the "Everlasting Father" (Isaiah 9:6), never leaving us or forsaking us (Hebrews 13:5).

The Father of compassion is our "abba," our "daddy" (Romans 8:15), providing the kind of close, personal help that marks the best human fathers.

Indeed, we can send "praise to the Father of compassion" because when life breaks down, there is not one thing we need more profoundly than One who has concern and love and help for us wrapped up in His heart.

But wait! There's more. "Praise be," Paul concludes, to "the God of all comfort."

God of creation. God of the Israelites. God of the new covenant. And thankfully, God of all comfort.

He made us.

He guided our story.

He provided life eternal.

And He comes beside us to put a cool cloth of comfort on our worried forehead.

He assures us of eternal life when death stares us down.

He calms us with His sovereignty when life seems out of control.

He soothes our damaged hearts when sadness wakes us in the morning.

Indeed, we "praise the God of all comfort."

One verse. Four titles.

One incredible, awesome God.

REFLECTION . . .

- What makes you stand in awe of God? His creation? His plan? His work in your life? His comfort?

- When has God comforted you the most? What does it mean to you that He is the "God of all comfort"?

DECISIONS, DECISIONS

What's behind it . . .

We sat, stunned, across the desk from a young man who was doing everything he could to help us. He was calm, polite, and exceedingly caring. Yet the task he was helping us accomplish could not have been made easy or pleasant no matter how he conducted himself.

We found ourselves in the office of a funeral home being asked the most out-of-place questions we had ever been asked. We had barely had a chance to pick ourselves up off the floor from the shock of Melissa's sudden, unexpected death.

We had just finished a private viewing of our once-vibrant teen's body in another section of this horrible place, and now we were expected to try to figure out how to memorialize a young woman who just hours before had been jet-skiing on Lake Michigan.

Our minds were still numb. Our eyes and our heads still hurt from endless tears and sobbing. And it didn't really feel like we were experiencing reality. This could not be happening.

"What kind of flowers do you want?"

"How about the program for the funeral?"

"Have you picked out a cemetery?"

He had to ask the questions, but why did he have to ask them of us? What had just happened? How could life have gone so awry?

Stunned, we stumbled our way along as we began a new existence, one with just a sliver of realization that what we were to say and do regarding our daughter's death could have an impact on others. For now, it was hard to see past our despair. It was hard to wrap our minds around a concept that would later bring us at least some hope: Melissa's life was in control of a sovereign and loving God.

GOD'S WORD ON IT . . .

Now listen, you who say, "Today or tomorrow we will go to this or that city, spend a year there, carry on business and make money." Why, you do not even know what will happen tomorrow. What is your life? You are a mist that appears for a little while and then vanishes. Instead, you ought to say, "If it is the Lord's will, we will live and do this or that."

James 4:13–15

SERIOUS CONTEMPLATION . . .

The sudden and unexpected death of a child leaves a family with a host of decisions that they had never given one second of thought to before. Life leads to decisions about schooling and clothes and music tastes and vacations.

Death leads to decisions about gravesites and caskets and obituaries.

So, on June 7, 2002, Sue and I found ourselves in a place we never imagined in our worst dreams we would be—sitting in the office of a funeral home, writing Melissa's obituary.

Her obituary! She was just seventeen. She was just learning to live. She was just beginning to become the woman she felt God wanted her to be. Obituaries and teenagers aren't supposed to go together.

Her obituary? What can you say in one column that appears in the most depressing section of the newspaper to encapsulate the beauty and wonder that was your vibrant young daughter's life? How can you do her any kind of justice with cold, dark words on a piece of newsprint? How do you testify to a community while your broken heart can hardly keep your shattered life alive?

As I sat contemplating how to tell the world about my precious daughter, one word came to my mind above all others: sovereignty. To my wife and me, God's sovereignty had to be at the top of any list of words that could explain Melissa's death.

In these opening moments of our sad new life without Melissa, I had to have assurance that this God we had loved and served and studied about and worshiped had been paying attention at nine p.m. on Thursday, June 6. We had to know that God had not misplaced Melissa momentarily that night. We had to have the reassurance that He had superintended her death and that He had been waiting in open-armed joy to receive her as she entered His kingdom.

Without sovereignty—without God's active role as the controlling figure in this tragedy—where else could we possibly go in our thinking?

Without sovereignty, there was only randomness. And not just with Melissa's death, but with all of our existence.

Or chaos.

Or maybe something worse. Maybe it could have been God's inability to act—that Melissa's death was out of God's hands. Without sovereignty, we would be left contemplating a surprised God unable to intervene in a terrible, horrible accident. Without sovereignty, Melissa's death would have been, to us, either the worst mistake God ever made or proof that there are some situations over which God has no control.

Everything we ever knew about God, however, indicated that this was simply not the case. We don't call Him the Almighty because He is incapable or limited. We don't worship Him as "King of kings and Lord of lords" because He is subject to some other power in this universe. We don't call Him Alpha and Omega, the beginning and the end, because He has somehow fallen asleep at the controls in the middle of things. No, He is the Creator, the Ruler, and the Sustainer of all that is. And if He is all those things—and we are convinced that He is—then He had to be alert and paying attention to the events of what, from this side of heaven, appeared to be an avoidable error.

So—clinging to God's supreme authority and power in this world—we began Melissa's obituary with these words: "By God's sovereign and loving hand, Melissa Ruth Branon . . ."

Since Melissa's death, I have found myself to be like a radar detector for any mention of the concept of sovereignty. My ears perk at any mention of God's role in life's events. Songs that speak of our heavenly Father's hand on our lives get played over and over on my CD player. It has become essential to grasp the difference between a life that is considered to be snuffed out suddenly without purpose or reason and a life that was taken from us under the caring, watchful eye of a God with a plan.

And it is a great comfort to know that God's loving control of Melissa's life was operational right up until the time He took her home.

How is tomorrow looking? Got plans?

Don't forget to say, "If it is the Lord's will, we will live and do this or that." There is assurance, hope, and comfort in those words, for they guide us to recall God's hand on our lives.

REFLECTION . . .

- When has God's sovereignty comforted you? When have you found it helpful to realize that God has things in His control?
- What do you have planned for tomorrow? Think of tomorrow as God's day to do with it as He wills. Then plan what you think He wants you to do.

THE BIG UNANSWERABLE

What's behind it . . .

Here are some situations that continue to make me think of this question: Why?

On September 11, 2001, some friends of ours lost their young married daughter, Lindsay, in a car accident as she was driving home from a prayer meeting for our country in the wake of the sad events of that day. To further complicate the why: she was pregnant; she had recently reconciled with God; she was killed in front of her parents, who were driving along behind her; and she was killed by a man on drugs. Why, indeed?

Another couple we know lost their preteen daughter, Heather, to a sudden onset of juvenile rheumatoid arthritis. It blazed into a full-fledged disease and took her life in a matter of days.

A twelve-year-old girl was practicing softball. Maggie was playing first base when a throw grazed off her glove, hit her in the neck, and killed her.

Another girl, Brianna, who was blind, attended a camp with other kids who had the same disability. While at the camp, the kids went swimming—and Brianna drowned.

Each of these families is a Christian family. Each of these girls had trusted Jesus as Savior.

Why? How can we not ask the question?

GOD'S WORD ON IT . . .

I trust in God's unfailing love for ever and ever.

Psalm 52:8

SERIOUS CONTEMPLATION . . .

We can understand the sovereignty.

We can grudgingly grasp the rights of the Almighty over everything.

We can make sense out of the centrality of God in our world.

But we are still left with the Big Unanswerable Question. *Why?*

God, there were other ways. Your name could have been glorified in ways other than her funeral and memorials.

We could have sensed your sovereignty in more normal situations. We wouldn't ever have doubted that you were in sovereign control of her life had things turned out differently.

The loved ones we have lost could have continued to glorify you with their life as you've asked them to do in their death.

So we still stand in bewilderment, God, at the most nagging and inglorious question we can imagine.

Why?

Why, when Christian young people are living for you, do you take them and leave behind the millions their age who snub their noses at you?

Why, when you knew how fragile the families left behind would be, did you steal them away?

Why, when parents invest so heavily in their children's lives, do we not get to see the dividends for just the few short years that intervene between now and eternity?

Why, God?

At our daughter's funeral, our friend and former pastor Dr. James Jeffery addressed that monstrous question. He said, "If you knew why God took Melissa, would it make it any easier to bury her?"

Jim's logic is inescapable. Indeed, even if God had written His reasons across the gloomy June sky above our church on the day of Melissa's funeral, that knowledge couldn't have undone reality.

Asking why is second nature to those who grieve or suffer through other of life's serious difficulties, even though we know we cannot get the answer here, nor would getting the answer heal the crack in our heart.

We keep asking this question, in one sense, because we do trust God. We trust that He is the controller of all that happens to us and therefore is responsible when struggles land in our path. And if He is responsible, we assume God had some reason for sending us this trial. That reason, if we knew it, would not lend any more importance or purpose to what is so inexplicable.

For a long time after Melissa died, I imagined that when we arrive in heaven, there would be a long line under a huge flashing sign that says, "Why?"

I envisioned shorter lines all over heaven.

"Talk to Paul" one would read.

"Sing with David" would be another.

Maybe there would be "Creation Questions Answered by Moses." But in my mind's eye I could see that the lines waiting under those signs would be miniscule compared with the long line stretching into eternity under the "Why?" sign.

"Why did my parents divorce?"

"Why was I so ugly?"

"Why didn't Someone heal my dad?"

"Why was my family so poor?"

"Why was I so mistreated as a child?"

"Why was there so much suffering in the world?"

But as I contemplated that question over and over and anticipated the day when I might get my answer from God himself, I began to dismiss my silly notion of heaven's *why* line—for two reasons.

First, as I thought about what I already knew about heaven, I decided that once we have entered heaven's reality, our glorified minds will suddenly be equipped with any information we need to know. Heaven, I decided, will not be a place for sighing and sadness as we relive the trouble and tragedies of earth. It will, instead, be a place of worship. Reunited with our loved ones, we'll join them in the worship of God that they will have already been enjoying. *Why* won't matter because what we will be doing will be what matters—and what we will then know will eliminate the retrospective sorrow that now clouds our lives.

And there is a second reason the *why* question has lost some of its compelling, overwhelming influence on my thinking. I have decided that I think I know the answer—or at least I know of an answer that, while not all-encompassing, does offer hope amidst the pain.

My daughter died for the same reason God brings anything into our lives—both things we wish for and those we wish hadn't happened. In reality, the *why* answer that causes some hope for my heart is the *why* answer even for our existence.

Tragedy comes so God's name can be glorified.

I must admit that I am not happy with this answer, because in my human, finite way of looking at things, Melissa's life, not her death, would have been a much better way of bringing glory to God.

However, we do not have the option of considering God's workings as an either-or situation. I cannot say that God can work only in the way I want Him to. And because of God's sovereignty, I do not have the right to suggest that my vision for Melissa's missing future was the better plan. Better for me, it would seem. Better for my family, we think. But somehow in God's mysterious dealings, truly not the best.

So now I am left with a choice. I can continue to trust God and then trumpet His greatness through recounting Melissa's life, or I can repair to a caved-in world of ongoing pain and hopeless musings about what could have been.

As Melissa's dad, I always felt I knew what was best for her. That makes it doubly hard to turn over the awful realities of her absence to Someone else. It is a painful, frightening thing I do when I release Melissa and suggest that the *why* of her death finds its answer in a positive outcome.

Yet I must. Against a heart crying, "No!" and a life seeking solace, I must release my child to God's sovereignty, to His plan, to His ultimate glory.

And in so doing, I move a step closer to returning to the arms of our heavenly Father.

REFLECTION . . .

- What have you had to turn over to God's loving hand—even if you didn't quite understand why this thing was happening?
- What is your top question regarding God's mysterious ways? Maybe it's not *why*. Maybe it's something else.

A COMPLETE LIFE

What's behind it . . .

On occasion, I'll get a letter from someone who wants to help me out regarding Melissa. This person has read my articles about Melissa's death, and he or she wants to fill me in about the reason Melissa died.

I have long since given up on trying to figure out why people do this—as if they have a special revelation that I've somehow missed. But I do realize that they are trying to help.

Regarding the hopefully helpful letter writers, the suggested reason that I dislike the most goes something like this: "Melissa died because God was protecting her from problems she might have in the future." I don't like this for a couple of reasons. First, it suggests what I don't want suggested: a life of trouble for my daughter. And second, it violates the truth of God's control.

Melissa's life was complete when she died. Some unwritten chapters were not out there waiting to be completed—maybe bad chapters with nasty things poised to happen. That's not the way it works.

There is comfort in this truth for me, as this devotional explains.

GOD'S WORD ON IT . . .

Man's days are determined; you have decreed the number of his months and have set limits he cannot exceed.

Job 14:5

SERIOUS CONTEMPLATION . . .

During the winter after Melissa's death, I was sitting at a school event with one of Melissa's good friends, Tara. This young woman had been among those girls Melissa made sure was included in group activities. A bit shy, Tara could easily have stayed on the fringe of high school life—except for Melissa. Mell made sure Tara was included.

On the day of Melissa's death, Tara had taken Melissa to the beach in her car. Then she had taken her to the cottage in her car. But then she turned Melissa over to Mell's boyfriend Jordan for the trip home.

As Tara and I talked about Melissa on that cold winter's night, she turned to me with tears in her precious eyes and said, "Mr. Branon, I wish I had taken Melissa home that night instead of Jordan."

I looked at this sweet teenager with such a tender heart and said, "Tara, if you had taken Mell home, you would have been in an accident."

Obviously, I am not clairvoyant, and I cannot hang my theological hat on this as a hard and fast truth, but Tara knew what I meant. I have grown to believe that there was nothing anyone could have done that night to prevent Melissa's death.

We can find evidence that God's hand controls the events of our lives by examining the words of Paul, who explained to the people of Ephesus that God "works out everything in conformity with the purpose of His will" (Ephesians 1:11). There is a divine pattern to the often-chaotic events of our lives, and while we may not be privy to how that pattern will eventually unfold, we know that God doesn't have to use an eraser on it. Each new event is designed as a part of that total pattern, and each event fits into the ultimate, completed picture.

More specifically, we know that each life God designed was on His drawing board for a purpose. And each day of that life was designated as important and pertinent to His plan. Psalm 139:16 tells us,

> *All the days ordained for me*
> *were written in your book*
> *before one of them came to be.*

In God's mysterious yet perfect plan, He gives us each an appointed amount of time on this earth. He has written the book of our life, and He knows how many pages that book contains—and there are no surprise endings to Him. When that final page is written, God superintends the end of that earthly life and, for the Christian, the beginning of a heavenly existence.

Other passages of Scripture seem to verify the concept that each of us has been assigned a length of time on this earth—a length that is part of God's distinctive plan for each of us. In Job 14:5, the great sufferer said this: "Man's days are determined; you have decreed the number of his months and have set limits he cannot exceed." The psalmist as well understood God's hand of control in matters of life and death. Directing his conversation toward God, David said, "Show me, O Lord, my life's end and the number of my days" (Psalm 39:4).

Whether it is my niece, who died just hours after she was born; my wife's grandmother, who lived to be 104; my teenage daughter; or your loved one who is too early gone—it is not the length of life that is most important (and believe me, it's an immense struggle to admit this truth). What is important is that God has His hand of control on that life.

I have to believe that God gave Melissa just seventeen years, ten months, and sixteen days to make a difference on this earth. She successfully fulfilled her mission, and on June 6, 2002, God called her into His presence. The last page of her book was written that day, and then God ushered her into His glorious presence.

We were shocked, stunned, and saddened by this sudden end to a remarkable young life, but we are in part comforted to know that Melissa does not get an incomplete in the grading scale of life. She had finished her race. She had run well. She was surely greeted by God's "well done" as she entered the awesome and unspeakable glories of heaven.

God is in total control of our days. We cling to that truth, not because it makes us miss the departed ones any less but because it helps us step back into the loving arms of a loving, comforting, merciful God.

REFLECTION . . .

- How does recognizing God's control on your life or on the life of someone you love help you when trouble comes?
- How do we deal with the word *accident*? Are the events that seem to occur randomly (a building collapses; a train jumps the track; a child gets hit by a misthrown softball or baseball) still under God's control?

RANDOM ACT?

What's behind it . . .

Melissa was indeed a precious gift from God, and we loved her with an unending, unconditional love. We guided her to God, knowing that the most important decision she would ever make would be to put her faith in Jesus.

We watched her turn from a painfully shy little girl who had to be held back from starting kindergarten because the teachers feared she wasn't ready to interact with other kids into a beacon of joy for her friends.

We protected her. We trained her. We smothered her with love—as did her brother and sisters. She grew up secure in our love and in God's care.

We entrusted her into that care, looking forward to what God might have in store for her as His child and as one who sought to honor Him.

But then came the call. The empty arms. The broken heart. The shattered family. God, what have you done?

GOD'S WORD ON IT . . .

Trust in the Lord with all your heart.

Proverbs 3:5

SERIOUS CONTEMPLATION . . .

As much as I believe the truth of God's sovereignty, I cannot say that I am happy about what it means. Yes, I can believe that Mell had an appointment with God in heaven on June 6, 2002, and yes, I can take some measure of comfort in knowing that her death was not random and meaningless in God's economy, but that does not mean I am pleased about it.

That God can superintend our conception, birth, and death is clear. Yet, there's another part of this equation that continues to trouble us.

How could He? Yes, He has the power, but there is something about His swooping down and intercepting our daughter that makes me ask, "How could you?"

How could a loving God do something that will for the rest of our lives bring ongoing sorrow and pain?

The death of a family member casts a dark pall on life. Heaven's rich gain is a family's deep loss, and the brightest day of the bereaved families' lives are tinted with an unpleasant gray.

Indeed, answering the question of sovereignty raises other questions about God that are nearly as unanswerable. Among those is this query, one that we posed to our former pastor shortly after we buried Melissa. Sue and I both were burning in our hearts to know what to think about a question that was troubling us greatly.

James Jeffery had been our pastor for several years. We had developed a unique relationship with him, and for the first time in my life I had developed a true friendship with my pastor. He was "Jim" to me, and that meant we could share on a different level. However, he had left our church a few months before Melissa died and was serving as a college president in Pennsylvania at the time of her death. I was hesitant to ask him to come back to perform Melissa's funeral, but when I did, he was more than glad to do so. We were honored and grateful.

When Jim stopped by our house shortly after the funeral, we knew that we could depend on his deep wisdom and his close, personal relationship with God. We knew we could ask him the really tough questions, and he would gladly attempt to answer them with a sincerity that we cherished and a love that warmed our hearts.

On behalf of Sue and myself, I posed the question.

"Jim, if someone had come into our home in the middle of the night and killed Melissa, we would have so much hatred for that person in our hearts. We would be so angry with that person for robbing her from us. We would want the full extent of the law to come down on his head, and we would have a hard time allowing for any mercy for him. He would have stolen our most precious possession, and we would expect eye-for-an-eye justice. In our theology, we say that God is responsible for Melissa's death. Why, then, if it is not okay for a murderer to take Mell's life, is it okay for God to?"

With the confidence of a man of God, Jim did not flinch from our question. Instead, he calmly and forcefully told us, "Because only God has the right to."

Perhaps this goes even deeper than the question of sovereignty. It goes to ownership and creatorship. It reminds us that our very existence is a gift from God's hand. As our Creator-God, He has the ultimate right over our every breath. We may live sometimes as if God is not even around, but in reality it is only by God's permission, power, and provision that we can even hope that our heart beats one more time.

After Jim made that simple yet profound statement about God's right over us as our creator and sustainer, he offered a challenge. He told us that the key step that we would have to take would be to trust God again—to put ourselves back into His hands and tell Him that we would trust Him to do what He had to do.

To be honest, this is where things get very, very difficult. We had trusted God. We had entrusted our children to His invisible greatness. We had prayed for protection for Melissa and all of our children. Yet she was gone.

And now we were to trust Him again?

Our heart cries out that we cannot. Yet our faith tells us that we must. To trust again—to give up our rights and to surrender to God, a God of unfathomable love and infinite knowledge—that is a key to restoring our relationship with Him. Slowly that task turned from impossible at first to a growing agreement that if we are to live again, we must trust again.

REFLECTION . . .

- What has happened in your life that makes it hard to trust God again? What are some small steps you can take as you try to return to His loving arms?
- What does it mean that God has ownership of us? Does that bother you, or make you feel comforted and protected?

CHAPTER
TWO

I SHALL NOT WANT

Sure, we will have needs. Indeed, days will come when our provisions will feel insufficient, when our wants will seem overwhelming. During those times— moments when we are at our weakest—we have the promise that the One who created this world and breathed His very life into us can meet our every need.

WANTS AND PROMISES

What's behind it . . .

One of the most joyous times of giving Melissa what she wanted came when she was sixteen years old. At the time, we were up to our ears in tuition payments—hers and Steve's for the Christian high school they attended, Julie's for the Christian college she was going to, and even some leftover loans for Lisa, who had already graduated from college.

So there wasn't a lot of money lying around the house waiting to be spent on a car for Melissa. And frankly, she didn't really expect one. But for convenience and to reward her for her diligence and respectable lifestyle, I decided to get her one.

Our school had an auction, and one of the items in the auction was a shiny, old Chevrolet Beretta parked out front of the school. I decided going into the auction that I would pay two thousand dollars for this well-used car. I had never entered an auction, so I didn't really have much savvy to work with.

When the bidding began, I somehow ended with an odd number—maybe $1,100. So another person made the bid when it got to $2,000. I had just a few seconds to decide: would I make it $2,100, or would I fold?

I decided to go for it. "Twenty-one hundred dollars!" I said. And the other bidder dropped out.

Melissa had a car. A rather beat-up one—but a car.

I don't recall Melissa ever being as excited about anything as she was about this car. She called her mom to spread the good news.

And as good as she felt, I felt better.

I had satisfied a want for my teenager. And it felt really, really good.

God, it appears in Psalm 23, likes to fulfill our wants too.

GOD'S WORD ON IT . . .

The Lord is my shepherd, I shall not want.

Psalm 23:1 KJV

SERIOUS CONTEMPLATION . . .

With one phone call and one funeral and one altered life, the promises of God developed a hollow sound. I saw the words. I knew what they said, but I began to wonder what they could possibly mean in this new chapter of our lives.

What do you do with the promise that if your children obey and live as they are supposed to, a long life is promised to them? How does that square with the reality of seeing your beautiful daughter lying in a casket as your friends and her friends, who knew what kind of girl she was, came by to cry with us. Wonder with us? Shake their heads with us?

And what about this promise, spoken by David in the most famous book of his grand cooperative work called the Psalms? David, troubled and sinful, yet great and powerful. A man who sinned greatly yet was still lifted up for his seeking of God's heart.

Whatever could the promise of Psalm 23 mean now that this Great Shepherd had somehow allowed one of His sheep—one of *my* sheep—to be taken from the flock?

"The Lord is my shepherd, I shall not be in want," David said, and we are expected to make this promise our own.

But I want. I want what I cannot have. I want what is utterly and unquestionably impossible to achieve.

I could want riches, and that would be possible. (Not probable, but it could happen.)

I could want happiness and joy, and, yes, despite it all, those two illusive life features could appear.

I could even want something big and glorious—such as world peace. And maybe God would make it happen on this side of eschatology, even if for just a little while.

But what I want the most escapes the realm of the real.

I recall a conversation with my wife about Melissa. In a moment of despair, she wondered aloud, "Why can't God make Melissa come back to life?"

That's the want I want.

But in this realm, in this life, that is not going to happen.

My sobbing at her gravesite will not awaken my daughter. My sitting on the grass above her head and talking to her can never cause her to shake free from the shackles of death and burst forth to brush away my tears. I am helpless to achieve what I want the most.

But the psalmist said, "I shall not be in want."

Should I stop this wanting? Should I deny my heart and bury my longings? Should I pretend that each waking hour is not filled with an unattainable desire?

To the psalmist, there seemed to be some connection between his ability not to want and his freedom to lie down in green pastures. Perhaps there, in those green pastures of total trust, the want goes away.

As I look for the green pastures, I conclude that they might be the quiet, calm evenings that my wife and I can spend together. They may be the family times when my kids and their spouses and their kids join Sue and me around the table and bask in the warmth of familial love and connectedness.

Yet even in these green-pasture experiences, I find the heavy sigh of sadness welling up in my chest. The joy of having my family around me accentuates the reality of an obvious but unmentioned absence.

I lie down in green pastures of speaking with God—of pleading with Him for calm and hope and peace. I look for the green pastures of connection by asking God in prayer to remind Melissa I love her and to tell her that He and I have just spoken.

In a hundred ways, I hope not to want—but I find myself stuck in the sorrow of death's reality.

This unavoidable tendency to want what I cannot have causes me to rethink this psalm, this promise—to find out for sure the connection between the shepherd, the green pastures, and the still waters. Intrinsic in the character of the Shepherd is something that is supposed to make me not desire the unattainable. Because the Lord is the Shepherd, there is expected to be something in Him that relieves the heart from the pain of expectations.

What is it? What about God as Shepherd can erase my wants even though all of my being tells me that I cannot be satisfied? What God-characteristics or God-actions will flip the switch on my inner being's got-to-have-it mechanism to stop it from the painful pursuit of the impossible?

In one tiny sense, I cannot want for my daughter any more than what she has. In a sense, she now has more than I could ever give her. She knows a joy and peace that a father can only dream of for his daughter. For her, I cannot possibly want anything greater.

As a father, I give up many things for my children's well-being. Dads know that it is not all about them. We grow accustomed to sacrificing for our children—in fact, we enjoy the trade-off of things in our lives in exchange for our children's happiness. And now, in a sense, I have given up my daughter so she could have ultimate joy and happiness. I don't have to want for her anymore. For that, I must give up my want—I must sacrifice my desire.

"The Lord is my shepherd; I shall not want" (KJV). For Melissa, there's nothing more I could want that she is not already enjoying.

"Dear Lord, please care for those we cannot throw our arms around. Please hold them close and reward them for their faith. Please let them know that each day on earth for us is a tribute to their lives. Please tell our loved ones how much we love them, and tell them that we are just a little jealous that although we may have known you for decades longer than they have, they know you in a way we cannot until the day we rejoin them and finally stand in your presence. And let them know that we are clinging hard to the hand of the One in whose presence they now bask."

This prayer helps us not to want so much anymore.

REFLECTION . . .

- What is your greatest want? How does "I shall not want" work into that deal?
- Read through Psalm 23 again and journal about how God is interacting with you throughout the elements of these verses.

ARE YOU CRAZY?

What's behind it . . .

One of my favorite prayer scenarios in the Bible takes place in the book of Daniel. Maybe you've been impressed by it as well.

It takes place in Daniel 9, and it gives me goose bumps to envision what happened. In verses 4 through 19, Daniel's understanding of God's plan spurs him on to prayer. He had read in the Holy Scriptures that the captivity that he was a part of would be over after seventy years. And since the seventy years of captivity were nearly over, Daniel wanted to remind God of His promise. So he did that in prayer. That's pretty cool on its own, because it reminds us that we can pray God's promises back to Him.

But here's the really incredible part. While Daniel was praying (v. 20), God sent the angel Gabriel on a nonstop flight to Daniel. Before Daniel even got done with his prayer, Gabriel was there with an answer.

Amazing! God can send us answers to prayer right smack in the middle of a prayer!

Then, in the New Testament, a similar thing happened. That's what the following devotional is about.

Could there be a pattern here? Prayer answers flying straight from heaven to our prayer room! For all of us who need God's hand in our lives to buoy us up as we trudge through the valley, these are some pretty encouraging stories.

GOD'S WORD ON IT . . .

Rhoda . . . exclaimed, "Peter is at the door!"
"You're out of your mind," they told her.

Acts 12:13–15

SERIOUS CONTEMPLATION . . .

Imagine having your prayer answered before your prayer session ends. That would be a boost to your faith, wouldn't it?

Peter was chained up in jail, and the future looked bleak. King Herod had already executed James, and Peter was scheduled for a public trial as soon as Passover was past. All Peter's friends could do was pray.

When that is all you can do—do you feel that it's enough?

Have you ever prayed diligently and with tears for a family whose little boy is dying of cancer—and you simply don't think he has, well, a prayer of surviving?

Have you ever prayed fervently that a family member would turn his or her life around before the pathway to obvious destruction swallows that person in irreversible tragedy?

Have you ever prayed wholeheartedly for a ministry that seems on the verge of losing its effectiveness because of struggles with finances or dissension or mismanagement?

Have you ever prayed your heart out for God to intervene, interfere, interrupt, or just enter the situation?

In these cases, it is not your own personal struggle that is tugging at your heart and forcing you onto your knees before God. While your own issues may still be pulling at your heart, you have decided to dedicate yourself to pleading with God for others. It is your love for someone else—your compassion for a person or institution you cherish—that has bowed your head and closed your eyes. It is your compassion that has spoken those words of intercession.

Trusting, you pray. You plead with God. You knock on His door and implore Him to act. You are, as the first-century church was doing for Peter, "earnestly praying to God" (Acts 12:5).

As we pray in these times of distress, are we preparing for God's answer? Are we anticipating that God will break through our muddled words and random thoughts with a response?

To our surprise, sometimes God says, "Yes!"

Imagine this happening. Imagine God acting on your prayer. The phone rings and your troubled loved one says, "I'm sorry. I'm coming back home." The e-mail announces that a jobless friend has been hired.

Do we tell the messenger, "You're out of your mind"?

Not always and probably not very often, God sends us direct answers before we can imagine the prayer has time to get registered in heaven. Are we trusting God with our prayers and waiting in hopeful anticipation for Him to break through when we least expect it?

REFLECTION . . .

- What is the hardest prayer request you have for God? Are you beginning to give up on it, or are you willing to keep knocking on His door?
- Have you ever experienced an "Are you crazy?" answer to prayer? Can that be a reminder that even in loss God is still at work?

GRACE ALONE

What's behind it . . .

God sent us Grace in more ways than one.

After we lost Melissa, we occasionally heard from her friends in various ways. But I think it was Grace—one of her classmates at school—who seemed to be there for us the most. True to her name, she was a sufficient friend, sending cards, writing notes on Facebook, and visiting when possible. Grace always seemed to have a word or a comment that lifted us.

Grace. Thank you.

And then there is the other grace. The grace God gives when we are at our weakest. It's funny that when we are weak and it would seem in our logical way God should send us strength—He sends grace.

Grace marks out the pathway to survival. It is all we need. And it somehow transforms weakness into strength.

Thank you, God, for both Grace and grace.

Both help us know how much you care.

GOD'S WORD ON IT . . .

My grace is sufficient for thee: for my strength is made perfect in weakness.

2 Corinthians 12:9 KJV

SERIOUS CONTEMPLATION . . .

Grace.

It all boils down to grace.

Grace is what makes life truly livable as we battle our way through the ups and downs, the peaks and valleys of our daily existence. Grace brings hope to hopeless situations. It provides light for dark days. It applies healing to broken hearts. It pours out understanding for the confused mind.

Grace, in fact, trumps the solutions we would seek when difficulties creep into our lives. Eager as we are to have our difficulties swept away so our pain can be relieved and we can relax in the comfort of an unburdened existence, we must recognize that the Master Designer of our lives sometimes sends grace as a sufficient substitute for pain relief.

Paul—faithful, dependable Paul—requested pain relief. He was being stuck in his flesh by a pointy thorn, and he wanted it gone. Like an ongoing, nagging irritant, this affliction was tormenting the apostle.

But God didn't pull out the thorn and toss it away. Instead, He sent grace—and He called it "good enough."

So what is this grace that God directs our way during times of distress and trouble? It is the free and undeserved favor He bestows on us.

Grace is the vehicle God uses to justify us at salvation (Romans 3:24). Grace trumps sin and its penalty.

Grace is what helps us stand in God's very presence (Romans 5:2). Grace provides peace in a world wracked by lawlessness.

Grace replaces the law in the new covenant (Romans 6:14). Grace relieves us of the harsh schoolmaster that is the law.

Grace is a source of God's riches (Ephesians 1:7). God didn't just give us a bit of grace; He "lavished" it on us, burying us in its richness and power.

Grace is a favor so effective in our lives that God can use it to displace our weakness with His unlimited power.

Think for a moment about the struggles that right now are burdening your life—the sadness or the emptiness or the despair that wake you up each morning. You are too weak in your own strength to conquer them alone.

And that is just where God wants you to be. When you are too weak, you have no choice but to trust the sufficiency of grace.

When tempted, we can "approach the throne of grace with confidence [God's confidence], so that we may receive mercy and find grace to help us in our time of need" (Hebrews 4:16).

When confused, we are not "carried away by all kinds of strange teachings. It is good for our hearts to be strengthened by grace" (Hebrews 13:9).

REFLECTION . . .

- How have you felt God's grace most clearly in your life of pain and struggle?
- Which of the characteristics of grace mentioned above have helped you the most as you have walked through your valley?

UP OR DOWN? WHICH IS IT?

What's behind it . . .

In Jamaica, the motto seems to be "No Problem, Mon." But as I studied Jamaica in preparation to go there with a high school chorale and preach at their Sunday meetings, I was struck by the reality that Jamaicans do have a multitude of problems.

Yet as I talked to the Jamaican people, I was hard-pressed to see why one of their difficulties is murder. Jamaica has one of the highest murder rates per capita in the world. However, the people are bright and friendly and so seemingly malice-free.

I wanted to remind them that no matter what the difficulty, we must continue to trust God. So the first time I preached in Jamaica, I would tell them of our tragedy, and then I would play Jeremy Camp's song, "I Still Believe."

Here's what the song says, in part:

> Though the questions still fog up my mind
> With promises I still seem to bear
> Even when answers slowly unwind
> It's my heart I see You prepare
> But it's now that I feel Your grace fall like rain
> From every fingertip washing away my pain
>
> 'Cause I still believe in Your faithfulness
> 'Cause I still believe in Your truth
> 'Cause I still believe in Your Holy Word
> Even when I don't see, I still believe

For my friends in Jamaica or for us wherever we live, the measure of our response to trouble comes down to those three words: "I Still Believe." If I don't, I throw away the remarkable words of 2 Corinthians 6:4–10 and all of the other hopeful words of Scripture.

GOD'S WORD ON IT . . .

As servants of God we commend ourselves in every way: in great endurance; in troubles, . . . in purity, understanding, patience."

2 Corinthians 6:4–6

SERIOUS CONTEMPLATION . . .

How bad are things, really?

Could it be that they are just as good as they are bad? Is it possible that the truest and best answer to our understanding of life's difficulties as a child of God is that He always gives provisions from His storehouse of riches to match the abundance of troubles we face?

It's a thought that began to form in my mind as I began to prepare some messages for a group of churches in a Caribbean nation that I knew was going through major economic and social difficulties. Here I was—the guy with the comfortable home and a good job—coming to their beautiful land to share with them about trouble and how to deal with it in a godly way.

While I know that our trouble—our heart-wrenching family tragedy—clearly rose to the level of a challenge to peace and joy in our lives, I also felt that perhaps my new friends in this sunny paradise could share with me sorrows on equal terms.

Then I read Paul's remarkable words in 2 Corinthians 6, and things began to clear up for me about this matter of living with hardships.

Our riches in Christ—our deep, abiding hopefulness in our earthly existence—come not from the nature of our circumstances or the fabric of our trouble. We are not rich or poor in Jesus because of some cosmic connection to sorrow or sadness. Our "up-ness" or "down-ness" depends not on whether our lives are filled with seeming blessings from God (wealth, ease, jobs, families, and the like) or whether they are bereft of outward evidences of blessings (poverty, trouble, joblessness, relationship problems, and the like). Our gauge of how good or how bad things are in life is this: do we recognize that the only richness that counts depends on our relationship with God?

Examine Paul's list of the ways we commend ourselves:

> *in great endurance;*
> *in troubles, hardships and distresses;*
> *in beatings, imprisonments and riots;*
> *in hard work, sleepless nights and hunger.*

At first glance, it appears that the way to reveal your God-heart is to get out there and get yourself into difficulty. The only good Christian is a beat-up Christian.

But Paul quickly changes gears. We also commend ourselves

> *in purity, understanding, patience and kindness;*
> *in the Holy Spirit and in sincere love;*
> *in truthful speech and in the power of God;*
> *with weapons of righteousness in the right hand and in the left.*

The bad life. The good life. The trouble we face. The good things we do. Up. Down. And Paul isn't done. We also commend ourselves

> *through glory and dishonor,*
> *bad report and good report;*
> *genuine, yet regarded as imposters;*
> *known, yet regarded as unknown; . . .*
> *beaten, and yet not killed;*

sorrowful, yet always rejoicing;
poor, yet making many rich;
having nothing, and yet possessing everything.

The riches of our lives are ledger-sheet-proof. We cannot add up our bank account and total God's blessings. He blesses the poor and the rich with the same grace. We cannot subtract our troubles and discount God's blessings. He blesses the brokenhearted and the untroubled with the same grace. We cannot figure our accounts with God on the basis of tangible goods or even intangible trials. Our wealth in the economy of God rises from His generous heart, and He bestows upon all of His people—whether they live in the poorest nation in the world or have suffered the worst tragedy in life—the incomprehensible riches of His love, His grace, and His kingdom.

Up or down? Whichever way you are feeling today, park yourself in Paul's world of wisdom and begin to understand the grand truth that as God's child you can have the joy of "possessing everything."

REFLECTION . . .

- Okay, which do you feel right now? Up? Down? How does it help to review Paul's teaching and to realize that God has given you an amazing array of blessings?
- Sometimes it is hard to appreciate intangible good things (God's blessings such as grace and peace)

when you are not experiencing tangible good things (monetary success, great relationships). Contemplate the difference and where you stand with this line of thinking.

THREE

HE LEADS ME

Lost. Directionless. Wandering. When we find ourselves enduring those moments, we cry out for One
who knows the path and has the end in view. Our
heavenly Father answers that cry. He guides. He
directs. Even in life's darkest moments, the One who
is the light leads us.

REMEMBERING THE GREAT SUFFERER

What's behind it . . .

Sometimes people say things that can be irritating to the sufferer—to the one who has suffered loss. In my experience, one
kind of these statements comes from well-meaning people who
are trying to practice empathy where it doesn't really apply.

For instance, on several occasions I have heard from folks
who have read about our loss of Melissa in *Our Daily Bread*
and then say something like this: "I know exactly how you
feel when you write about your loss. Recently, my dog died,
and I can't get over it."

While these people are kindly trying to show their concern, that kind of statement demonstrates why we do more harm than good sometimes by comparing our sadness with others'.

I am indeed sorry that those folks lost their cherished animal, but the comparison does not stand.

I always find it more helpful when folks say to me, "I heard about your daughter. I am so sorry. I cannot imagine what it is like."

That is so true. None of us can imagine the pain of another person.

Even a fellow father who has lost a teenage daughter will go through pain that is different from mine. Relationships are different. Circumstances are different.

I've thought a lot about this idea of comparative suffering.

Perhaps we need to go back to Jesus in our thinking about suffering, for surely He understood a kind of suffering that we will never know anything about. Let's see what He can teach us.

GOD'S WORD ON IT . . .

Therefore, since Christ suffered in his body, arm yourselves also with the same attitude, because he who has suffered in his body is done with sin."

1 Peter 4:1

SERIOUS CONTEMPLATION . . .

One thing that seems unbecoming for the struggling child of God is to compare our sufferings with those of others. While it may feel true that some things we endure appear to us to be far worse than what others have gone through, in reality this kind of weighing and measuring of trouble accomplishes nothing.

There is, however, one aspect of suffering-comparisons that can do us some good. That comes when we realize that what we have gone through for the cause of Christ and what Jesus went through for our cause can result in the very same attitude He had.

Think about what a gift that is! Jesus Christ, of course, suffered through something we cannot in our wildest imagination fathom. Although the movie *The Passion of the Christ* tried to capture for us the utter torture our Savior endured on that sad Good Friday, there is one aspect of His pain that we cannot grasp no matter what we see. We cannot comprehend the mental, spiritual, and emotional agony He endured.

When we suffer loss here on this earth—even if we suffer for the cause of Christ—we suffer for ourselves as individuals. Jesus, though, in the most miraculous experience of vicarious representation ever, suffered for every sin that was ever committed. Billions upon billions of sins were carried on His bloodstained shoulders that day. Inside Jesus' heart and mind, He knew what was happening. He recognized the weight, and He knew where it came from. The agony of that representative suffering must have been the most intense pain ever experienced.

But although we cannot possibly go through one single percent of Jesus' suffering, one aspect of His suffering that we can identify with is this: we can mirror His attitude. Peter suggested that our role as fellow sufferers with Jesus was not in the pain

He suffered but in the remarkable attitude He displayed. And that attitude was marked by a willingness to do God's will.

Think about that. Think about how that affects those of us who have struggled with some aspect of God's dealings that we have found not to our liking. God's will, it seems, is for us to endure, and our response, if we wish to honor our Savior and show trust in God, is to recognize the importance of suffering in God's economy. As difficult as it seems, it is our task to accept this suffering as our way of pointing others to God, which we know to be God's will for us.

When we remember the Great Sufferer, our proper response is to thank Him for His attitude and then pray that we can demonstrate a similar response to the people around us.

REFLECTION . . .

- In what way does Jesus' attitude of willingness to suffer for us help me when I think of what I have to suffer during this life?
- How can I use Jesus' example to encourage others— despite the fact that I sometimes struggle with circumstances about my life that I don't like?

THE PROMISE: TAKE WHAT YOU CAN GET

What's behind it . . .

Quite a few years ago, there was a major league baseball player named Dave Dravecky. He was a good, young lefthander who made the All-Star team and appeared to have a bright future. But then he got cancer in his pitching arm.

His career then took on the elements of an interesting drama instead of being simply a story of baseball. He seemed to conquer cancer and came back to pitch again. But in his second start after cancer treatment, he fired a fastball and broke his arm. He would never pitch again.

In fact, doctors decided that they would have to amputate his arm.

During the time of his illness and before the amputation, an odd thing happened that has always stuck with me. One day a guy showed up at Dravecky's door in Ohio. He had traveled hundreds of miles to reach Dravecky's house, and his message for Dave and his wife Jan was that if Dravecky would just have more faith, he would be healed.

Dave Dravecky is a man of immense faith, and for this person—as well-intentioned as he might have been—to do this was unconscionable. To impugn Dravecky's faith and to suggest that it was his lack of it that was the reason for his cancer was both theologically wrong and morally demeaning.

That incident to me has always stood out as the epitome of misunderstood faith—of not really grasping the entire counsel of God concerning the difficulties we face.

It's a subject we need to consider seriously as we deal with the rough road we must sometimes travel.

GOD'S WORD ON IT . . .

God is our refuge and strength,
an ever-present help in trouble.
Therefore we will not fear, though the earth give way
and the mountains fall into the heart of the sea.

Psalm 46:1–2

SERIOUS CONTEMPLATION . . .

Have you ever heard of revisionist history? That's what takes place when a so-called historian with a specific agenda bends the truths of history to make it fit his or her philosophy.

An extreme example is denying the fact that the Holocaust took place during World War II. Occasionally, a person with something against Jewish people, for instance, will claim that no Jews were exterminated during Hitler's reign—that the whole thing was made up.

As crazy as that sounds, it's not too much different from what we sometimes do with God's Word to us. We take the hard facts of Scripture and turn them around to match what we wish were true or what we would like to proclaim is true.

One example : those who would tell us sufferers that the reason for our struggles is that our faith is weak. God would eliminate our difficulty if we would just ratchet up our faith and believe harder, they say.

This portrayal of God as our Great Fixer of All Problems sounds great. What an amazing life this would be if God had told us He doesn't want us to face any kind of trouble and that He's right there to solve every problem.

History and the biblical record don't seem to support that.

Ever heard of Joni Eareckson Tada? Now there's a woman of faith—a pillar of godliness—a true servant of God. If faith and trust were the magic formula for relief from trouble, this is a woman whose disability should be fixed faster than you can say Joni and Friends.

She's a woman who struggled mightily against the prospects of disability when she was a young woman, yet now she faces her struggles with a grace and winsomeness that is a marvelous testimony to God's faithfulness despite her inability to walk.

Or what about Billy Graham? When old age set in to rob this great evangelist of his strength, imagine the millions who prayed for him. After all, his preaching led untold thousands to trust Jesus Christ, so you can imagine their prayerful concern. And the man himself, truly a humble man of faith, would be a candidate for an escape from physical trouble.

Yet he has never recovered from his life-sapping illness, and he has had to leave his public speaking ministry.

In the Bible, we see numerous examples of godly people suffering negative circumstances from which you might assume they would be exempt.

But let's look at just one: Jesus. Paul is a good example of this, but Jesus is better. Paul was good. Jesus was perfect. Paul served God. Jesus was God.

Jesus was the ultimate righteous man—the ultimate man of faith.

Yet he suffered. He faced trouble. In fact, He even asked God to get Him out of His most threatening trouble.

If Jesus—our Savior and our example—had to face blood-sweating difficulties in His life, if the man who is at the center of our faith had to endure hardships, who are we to think that we won't face troubles?

That's the hard fact. We cannot escape problems any more than Paul could escape his thorn in the flesh or Jesus could escape the agony and ignominy of the cross.

Anyone who says otherwise is revising truth into something less.

So what good did it do to establish this fact? Wouldn't we be better off not to know the impossibility of avoiding trouble?

Absolutely not. God did not exempt the faithful from trouble; He did something else—something more valuable than pain-free existence.

He offered to be our strength, our hope, our refuge.

He offered to take us under His mighty wings and provide needed help when trouble comes.

He offered to be our ever-present help, our continual, constant source of strength. In every second of every trial we face, we stand arm-in-arm with the God of all power. What we cannot stand to bear, we hand to Him. What we cannot understand, we entrust to Him. What we cannot come to grips with, we yield to Him.

Trouble. It will surely come. And the psalmist tells us that when it does, our "ever-present help" (v. 1) is "the Lord Almighty" (v. 7), for He "is with us" (v. 7). He is our "fortress."

Revisionism doesn't help—but God's presence does. Cling to Him.

REFLECTION . . .

- What has been the most erroneous spiritual advice you've ever received from someone who was "just trying to help"?
- Is there more faith in believing that we are immune to problems if we live right—or in trusting God completely that He always knows what He is doing even if things don't go our way? How have you seen the answer to this worked out in your life?

KEEP CALLING

What's behind it . . .

The first words my wife exclaimed upon hearing that Melissa was gone were these: "The pain is too great to bear." I will never forget those haunting words from my best friend.

In that moment there was an emptiness and a feeling of despair that I cannot even describe. It was a feeling of being beyond help. Body, soul, and spirit all were devastated beyond imagination.

Agony prevailed, and darkness surrounded us.

"A pain too great to bear." What in the world could we do? All that was left was to cry out to God.

Where does that cry go? When the bearing of the pain sinks us into a pit of agony, what can we expect to happen with our cry for assistance? How does it escape the pit, reach God's ears, and signal the needed help?

GOD'S WORD ON IT . . .

Then you will call, and the Lord will answer; you will cry for help, and he will say: Here am I.

Isaiah 58:9

SERIOUS CONTEMPLATION . . .

Jesus' haunting words on the cross break our hearts. In pain. Burdened by millions of sins. Hanging humiliated in front of friends and foes alike, Jesus used nearly the last measure of His waning energy to shout, "My God! Why have you forsaken me?"

We can hardly bear the thought—God turning His back on His precious, sinless only Son.

Forsaken.

By God.

Have you ever felt as if you were there?

Touched by trouble, you have cried out to the Lord, pleading for help.

Perhaps your family has been overtaken by financial burdens that threatened to sweep away your dreams.

Perhaps you have been misunderstood and mistreated by someone you trusted, sapping the hope from your life and the joy from your future.

Perhaps life itself has lost its appeal, and you simply don't know how you could again think a happy thought.

In agony of spirit, you have cried out to God. You have pleaded with Him for help.

And you have felt like Jesus. You have felt as if God has forsaken you, that He doesn't care, or that He has been reserving His blessing and attention for someone else.

This cannot be true.

In multiple ways, God has reminded us that He is there for us when we need Him most.

In Isaiah, the prophet told the people, "The Lord will answer; you will cry for help, and He will say: Here am I."

The "here am I" of God's promise is all you need. It is a "here am I" of provision, of compassion, and of love.

In 2 Chronicles, Solomon testified that even if the problems we face are of our own doing, and, as a result, heaven itself is shut off from us, our turning from our error, our humility, and our prayer for help will result in a message from the very portals of heaven itself.

The "I will hear from heaven" promise gives direction for repentance and expectation of God's forgiveness.

In Exodus 2:24, Moses exposed God as a compassionate heavenly Father who listens to His people's groans—and offers them deliverance that corresponds to His promises.

Do you feel that your prayers are being offered in a sound-proof booth? That your pleas for His help are like shouting into the wind? That your prayers are all ending up in heaven's dead-letter office? Not true.

Keep calling. Keep listening. Keep examining God's Word to us.

God is there. And He hears.

REFLECTION . . .

- What is influencing you to stop calling on God? What pain is too much for you to handle—so much that you think about not praying?
- When have you called on God and found the hope and help you needed? Contemplate again the great feeling that was for you.

THE WEEPING ONE

What's behind it . . .

A few weeks into our story of grief, my son Steve and I began to go back to the Sunday morning service at our church. Of course things were far from the same as they had been before. The reasons are obvious, and I really don't need to spell them out.

But because things were different, we would sneak into church a little late and settle in just a few rows from the back.

Right away we would be thrust into the song service, and right away a problem would ensue. I could not make it all the way through the songs without breaking down. I would stand there with tears running down my cheeks and with my shoulders shuddering.

Steve would lean over to me and say, "Dad, stop it. You're embarrassing me."

Well, I was embarrassing me, too. But I couldn't stop it. The songs always made me think of Melissa in one way or another, and inevitably I would cry.

To be honest, I cry too easily.

Sometimes it has nothing to do with Melissa. It might even be a bunch of athletes who are ecstatic over winning a championship. Or maybe it's some YouTube presentation like that Scottish woman, Susan Boyle, who impressed even Simon Cowell on *Britain's Got Talent*.

That's one reason I love the fact that Jesus wept. I love the fact that my Savior, like me, can be brought to tears. It makes me feel not quite so alone as a male who can get a little emotional. Jesus was a man's man who withstood amazing challenges—yet He was also a man with a soft heart.

We often concentrate on all the heroic characteristics of our Lord. But for just a few minutes, let's see what it means that He could be reduced to tears.

GOD'S WORD ON IT . . .

When Jesus saw [Mary] weeping, and the Jews who had come along with her also weeping, he was deeply moved

*in spirit and troubled. "Where have you laid him?" he
asked. "Come and see, Lord," they replied. Jesus wept.*

John 11:33–35.

SERIOUS CONTEMPLATION . . .

Power. Majesty. Wisdom. That's Jesus. *The power* to create
the world and all that is in it. *The majesty* of One who shared
God's glory in heaven and who will one day sweep back to
earth in a spellbinding display of rescue. *The wisdom* of the
One who confounded the teachers with His wondrous proc-
lamations during His earthly sojourn.

Jesus is power and majesty and wisdom.

And oh, yes—tears.

More than once while Jesus dustied His sandals walking
the pathways of Galilee, He was reduced to tears by what He
saw. Jesus was not only the Man of Sorrows, He was a man
who sorrowed. The great God of the universe was not above
being a man of compassion when a friend died or when a city
touched his heart.

Think of what this means to each of us as we travel the
rough road of life's surprising struggles. Jesus—our pattern for
life, our example of goodness—has endorsed tears. The One
who built us an eternal home that will be tear-free has given
us permission to express our sadness while on this earth.

This man had shown that He was a great physician by
healing the blind. He had demonstrated that he was a great
provider by feeding the five thousand. He had displayed

diplomacy by dealing perfectly with the sinning Samaritan woman in a remarkable cross-cultural confrontation.

Jesus had built quite a reputation as He made His way through the countryside. And as that reputation continued to soar, what possible advantage could there be for Him to cry— to show what most would perceive as a weakness? Why would the man who could fix anything ever be reduced to allowing salty tears to streak His glorious face?

And there's something else. Read the story of Jesus when He visited Mary and Martha, whose brother Lazarus had just died.

Jesus was going to heal Mary's brother anyway.

This was not a situation where the despair of death would seem to have its usual stranglehold on emotions. In a sense, it would seem that Jesus' tears were not needed since He could undo the reason for the sadness anyway.

Yet the tears—unnecessary in our estimation or not— show Jesus' heart. He feels the pain we feel. His heart sorrows with our hearts. Eventually, He's going to wipe the slate clean for every one of His children, yet even as we suffer on this planet, He looks at us with compassion.

He is the Son of the Father of all comfort, and there is not one element of our sadness that escapes His attention. It would appear that Jesus' tears were tears of empathy—tears that said to Mary and Martha, "Because you hurt, I hurt."

Elsewhere in Scripture we are told to cast our burdens on the Lord for He cares for us. He cares enough to cry. When our struggles grab us and threaten to rob us of the energy of life, we need to turn to Jesus and see that He cares enough to cry.

He's powerful. He's majestic. He's wise. And he's compassionate.

There is no better person to turn to when trouble interrupts our life than One who has the power to deal with the problems and the compassion to cry about them as well.

REFLECTION . . .

- What about Jesus' tears speaks most to you when you struggle with a life problem?
- Many see tears as weakness in a person. What proves to you that Jesus' tears were not a sign of weakness but of power?

CHAPTER
FOUR

HE RESTORES MY SOUL

During life's most difficult days, the pain can be so intense that it feels like our soul is suffering. Our inner life feels crushed. Defeated. On life support. That's when the Great Physician wields His healing power, restoring our soul and reminding us that with Him all things are possible.

WHAT HAVE I DONE?

What's behind it . . .

Whenever I think about the messes Christians get themselves into, I can't help but be reminded of the football player who fumbled his testimony on the night before the Super Bowl.

The loss this man suffered in testimony and reputation has taken many years to overcome—with man that is. I wonder, though—if he repented immediately—if he got right back in good graces with God long before he did with other Christians.

The man won an award for being an exemplary Christian on the morning before the Super Bowl.

Then on the night before the Super Bowl he got arrested.

On the day of the Super Bowl, his story was an embarrassment for the people who gave the award and for Christians everywhere.

Surely he must have kicked himself and said, "What have I done?"

His indiscretion was public. Ours, not so much.

But we need to know how to get out of the slimy pit. We all slide down there from time to time.

GOD'S WORD ON IT . . .

I waited patiently for the Lord;
  he turned to me and heard my cry.
He lifted me out of the slimy pit,
  out of the mud and mire;
he set my feet on a rock
  and gave me a firm place to stand.

Psalm 40:1–2

SERIOUS CONTEMPLATION . . .

It doesn't take much.

Just one little indiscretion. Perhaps it appears to be a little sin at first—one that you figure you can wiggle out of if it gets discovered.

But then it leads to another. And another.

Little lies become whoppers. Seemingly little sins become monsters.

A tiny puddle of bad decisions becomes a raging torrent of trouble.

And soon you've got yourself into a hole so big it feels as if a giant crane couldn't pull you out of it.

This, my friend, is the other side of trouble.

The kind of trouble we get ourselves into while wearing the cloak of Christianity in order to insulate us from those we don't want to disappoint.

Dreams are dashed. Reputations are ruined.

And that once-little indiscretion has taken you down as you sit in the dark with your head buried in your hands saying, "What have I done?"

Embarrassed. Discredited. Hopeless.

Not necessarily.

Not necessarily hopeless.

You are walking in David's shoes right about now. You've done the terrible deeds. You've been found out. Your kingdom lies crumbling at your feet.

But you look back over your shoulder at the once great king and you notice that the bad beginning of his indiscretion did not lead to a hopeless ending. You listen to the apostle Paul's surprising words about this man who committed the vilest of sins against two families—his and Bathsheba's, and you are surprised.

You are shocked because what you've noticed most often about Christians is that they shoot their wounded. But as you sit in your sadness and look for a way out, you need a reminder that your life is not in the hands of tut-tutting others but in the hands of an inexplicably forgiving God.

Back to Paul and his surprising proclamation.

What is surprising about what the apostle called the adulterous murderer named David?

In Acts 13:22, he said that God "testified concerning him, 'I have found David son of Jesse a man after my own heart.'" Thousands of years after David's sin, Paul was inspired to repeat the predictive words of 1 Samuel 13:14 concerning the future king.

How could this be? How could David still be worthy of such acclaim after what he did?

It's all God.

Listen to David as he recounts God's incredible forgiveness. In Psalm 40, the king shares with us what happened.

First, David "waited patiently for the Lord." David was remorseful. He was sorry. And he told God about it.

And look what God did. He looked down and saw that David—His handpicked leader of His handpicked people—was immersed in a pit full of slime, muck, and mire.

The perfect, almighty, majestic God reached down His hand of forgiveness and drew David, dripping with filth, out of the pit, setting him up on a solid rock and putting in his mouth a new melody of praise.

Because of God's love and compassion, David the sinner became David the example, and, as a result of God's willingness to rescue him from the pit, others can look and live.

Perhaps you live in the mud hut of "What have I done?" You hide behind the door, knowing that you have sullied your name and God's. You have blown the confidence God placed in you when He drew you unto himself in the name of Jesus. You feel that your sin has cut you off from God and cast you as a spiritual loser.

Reach up. Find a window and extend your arm through it, allowing God in His mercy to grab your hand and pull you from your fortress of sorrow. He will wipe you off through His forgiveness. He will set you on the solid ground of His grace. And you will again be able to reflect His love to others.

You can be a person after God's heart—again.

REFLECTION . . .

- What is your route to the slimy pit? Is there something that you do that would embarrass you and your family if you were found out? Do you feel that God can help you with that?
- What if you don't have a hidden sinful behavior? What steps can you take to make sure you don't develop one?

A LITTLE HELP HERE!

What's behind it . . .

Have you ever tried to read the Bible through in the year using one of those little pamphlets that tells you how many chapters to read in one day? What happens when you get to

Chronicles? Or you have a couple of weeks full of meetings, kids' events to attend, or you are too sick to read? You get so far behind that you just can't catch up.

I remember one year when my wife was diligently keeping up her reading, and I kept getting farther and farther behind. I may have hung in there until April, but I got hopelessly lost in life's mundane activities. I felt awful because I really wanted to read the whole Bible that year.

Failing to follow through on a goal is a loss that all of us experience. It's not a huge loss, but it is irritating nonetheless. When we weigh it against some of the major troubles we face, it seems almost meaningless. However, in the interest of bettering ourselves and attempting to grow in grace and in the knowledge of our Lord, these failures can have debilitating consequences if we let them.

So let's get some help with this before we move on to more serious, more troublesome issues. Let's seek God's help as we set out to move ahead in our lives.

GOD'S WORD ON IT . . .

Have mercy on me, O God,
according to your unfailing love;
according to your great compassion
blot out my transgressions.

Psalm 51:1

SERIOUS CONTEMPLATION . . .

Did you ever wake up on the day after you made a resolution to follow God more diligently and realize that you've already messed up the plan?

You think, *What is the matter with me? I know I'm supposed to be following the What-Would-Jesus-Do? pattern, and I knew He never would have done what I did wrong yesterday.*

You kick yourself, realizing, *Hardly twenty-four hours have passed since I set out to be more godly, and I already blew it.*

Is this you? Do you stand before God, along with the rest of us, on the first day of a New-Me Venture with a tarnished slate?

For those of us who live in a world touched by tragedy or pain, it would seem that we would take extra care to avoid that kind of error—that we would do anything to live right.

After all, don't we sometimes think that if we live a godly life God will reward us by not visiting more pain upon us? That may be a theological question needing further pursuit, but for now it certainly sounds logical to strive for righteousness as we seek God's blessing.

Anyway, here we stand, blemished. Our resolutions for self-improvement are still fresh on our computer hard drive, and we've already violated the one that says, "Strive to be more godly."

- Maybe it was a harsh word to a relative who seems to always be the Scrooge to your Christmas.

- Maybe it was waking up today with the realization that your entire yesterday was used up without even talking to God or reading His Word.
- Maybe it was jealousy toward someone who has more, knows more, spends more, or has some other advantage.

Here's the good thing. No matter if we feel that we messed up on day 2 of a New-Me Venture or after three weeks of success, it's not too late to take care of matters the Psalm 51 way.

It's not too late to pull up a chair for a chat with God. "Father, I need a little help here. I kind of need your mercy. I need some of your unfailing love. I need a batch of your compassion. I have sinned, and I need you to blot it out. Forgive it. Bury it in the ocean where I can't find it again. Thank you."

See, life in the world of temptation is not unlike life in the world of trouble and pain. We need to ask God to forgive us when temptation to sin becomes sin—just as much as we need to ask God to come alongside and carry us when our trouble becomes too great.

When we need some help coping with a world that doesn't come out the way we want it to, or when we need help coping with life that doesn't come out the way He wants it to, God is there.

So get that assistance from God. Plead for His mercy and start again to attempt a life of daily dedication to God's ways. His mercy, unlike our faithfulness, will never run out.

REFLECTION . . .

- Yesterday, I didn't really see that problem coming. How can I better prepare myself to avoid this kind of thing again?
- How many times will God forgive me if I need His forgiving help again?
- Do I sometimes think that because I've suffered pain in my life, I'm immune to sin?

"WHERE IS YOUR GOD?"

What's behind it . . .

Loss and tragedy can drive us to God. But it can also drive us away from Him.

Over the years since I began writing about our family's grief, I've heard from families in which one or more members of the family rejected God after a death.

Sometimes, with the death of a child, one of the two parents will run completely away from our heavenly Father. That parent will conclude that if such an awful thing can happen to his or her child, then there cannot possibly be a God overseeing things.

We've seen a member of our family struggle with that question—actually turning his back on God and nurturing a feeling for hatred toward Him because of Melissa's death.

Thankfully, that has changed, but the reality is that loss can make even godly people question their faith.

This article came to mind after hearing a high school chorale directed by Melissa's sister, Lisa, sing a song that includes that mocking phrase, "Where is your God?" The song, of course, provides the answer as it reminds us of God's presence.

Maybe you have felt like this—that God in theory seemed like a good idea until something happened to make God in reality seem hard to grasp.

Consider the choice and the gravity of your decision: you can choose to trust the God of hope—or you sink into utter chaos. Choose hope, I say. Choose God.

GOD'S WORD ON IT . . .

My tears have been my food
day and night,
while men say to me all day long,
"Where is your God?"

Psalm 42:3

SERIOUS CONTEMPLATION . . .

They are out there. Relentless critics of the one true God. People who look at your situation and wonder how you can keep believing in God when your world is crumbling down around you.

Perhaps you've heard them whispering in your ear the kinds of ideas that ran through Job's mind: that it would be better to just curse God and die. Or worse, they come alongside you and jab you with questions like, "How can you believe in God when you have all this trouble?" Or "Why are you wasting your breath to cry out to someone who isn't even there?"

"Where is your God?" "Where is your God?" The angry crescendo builds in its mockery—and you have no answer.

You've cried out to Him. You've sought His solace and His intervention. And then the silence enveloped you like an evil cloud.

You begin to wonder to yourself, "Yes, God, where are you?"

If that has ever been you, follow the psalmist on his path to discovery—his road to righteousness and finally to the peace that only God can give.

He began with a picturesque image of the deer yearning for a drink of refreshing water—a deer on a single-minded mission to find an invigorating drink from a stream. Similarly, the psalmist said, his own soul thirsted for God.

It begins with a thirst—a desire to see God, to taste His precious presence. Yet in the middle of the search—a search punctuated by tears—came the siren songs of the doubting, the faith-robbing taunts of the unbelieving, asking that haunting question: "Where is your God?"

The psalmist pines for the long-past day when he led the worshipers into praising and glorifying God. His soul is downcast, yet he knows the solution; he knows the answer.

It is hope that leads to praise. It is remembering God. It is feeling the washing waves of God's great love sweeping over the beleaguered soul.

The anguished soul has God's love as his guide during the day and His song as a communication in the night. Like the children of Israel in days past, we can know that God's hand of direction never fails us.

Yet that taunting returns, those mocking voices asking about God and where He could possibly be.

And while He may not be there with the answer desired at the moment, something is offered that portends good things ahead.

Hope.

God offers hope where there is no hope. And hope is all one needs sometimes—the assuring knowledge that God is there and that He cares. And from that hope emits praise to the One who is called Savior and God.

"Where is your God?" He is always there. On the horizon. With His hand reaching out to offer hope, because He alone can save. He alone is almighty.

Pant for God—your only hope.

REFLECTION . . .

- Do I listen to the mocker's cry and begin to believe that God is somehow silent—hidden from my voice?
- What evidence do I have from Scripture or from life that the mocker's cry is not true?

HEART CRY

What's behind it . . .

There's a phrase that is sometimes suggested to those who struggle with loss but one against which we recoil. It's the concept of "getting over" the death or divorce or other circumstance.

One person was told that she would "get over" her daughter's death in six months.

To put it clearly and crudely: "That ain't gonna happen." There is really no "getting over" such circumstances.

Older women who have talked to me after speaking engagements have told me that they lost a child more than forty years ago. And they still cry out for that child. They still feel the agony.

The reality that "getting over" won't work, though, is not a reality that should stop us from going on. What we all need to strive for, instead, is finding God's word of hope in the midst of our struggle. That's what we find in this passage in Lamentations.

We lament, indeed. Our hearts hurt. But look at what God can do for us in the middle of that hurt.

GOD'S WORD ON IT . . .

This I call to mind
and therefore I have hope:
Because of the Lord's great love we are not consumed.
Lamentations 3:21–22

SERIOUS CONTEMPLATION . . .

In Lamentations, we find the heart-cry of a man who risked everything to stand up to people who didn't want to hear what he had to say—who threatened him with death when he told them about God's judgment for their wrongdoings. This man stuck his neck out for God as very few people ever do.

Yet look at how Jeremiah describes his relationship with God in Lamentations 3. The great prophet felt defeated by God's "arrows" (v. 12). He felt isolated from people because of his message (v. 14). And worse yet, he felt abandoned by God (vv. 15–20). No wonder he lamented.

Can you identify?

Look at verse 18. Do you want to sing along with the sad song of the abandoned? How many times have you echoed the sentiments in this verse? "My splendor is gone," said the prophet.

Indeed, because of the difficulties you've faced, how many times have you felt that life is "not much fun anymore"? Or how many times have you sighed that deep sigh of despair when awful reality again grips your heart?

I feel those things when I think of the magic of a child's smile, which is the splendor of a father's life. Seeing my daughter happily playing her heart out on the volleyball court made my soul leap for joy. Watching her as that shy smile of contentment crossed her face in grand moments of familial joy was a splendor unmatched by even the summer sun.

And now, that splendor cannot be recaptured.

But the prophet went on. For him, gone as well was all he "had hoped from the Lord."

It isn't much, really, that parents hope for. Children. Nurtured children. Happy children. A heritage of hope and joy that carries Mom and Dad through the hard times and makes the sometimes-challenging life as parents a thrill marked by occasional spills.

Yet hopes die easily when death comes to visit.

And hope's early demise turns a horizon of possibilities and promises into a valley of deep hurt.

Jeremiah, we understand. We feel the pain of your inspired words.

But we keep reading our way through the gloom of Jeremiah's complaint, just as in life we keep going through the fog of our pain.

Then, unexpectedly, a light shows through, a tantalizing glimmer from a word that has been so mysterious to us.

"I have hope," Jeremiah says.

Hope? How?

"Because," he says, "of the Lord's great love we are not consumed."

It's a reminder. It's a flashback to all that we've heard about God during our lives. His great love. God's great love. A reality that our greatest loss cannot erase.

A truth. A word from above.

A reminder that it is not our feelings that we are called to trust. It is not on our circumstances that we are required to rely. It is God. A God who has great love.

And compassion. His never-failing compassion.

Feelings overwhelm us. Feelings talk us out of joy. Feelings sneak around inside of us and destroy our contentment. Feelings come, feelings go.

But God's love keeps us from being consumed.

And His compassions do not fail. They visit us each morning if we let them.

And every morning, we have the opportunity to present our feelings—our feelings of unbearable pain—and turn them over to the One whose faithfulness is great.

These are not easy truths to accept. It is not painless to suggest that instead of clinging to sadness we should grasp God's love.

It almost feels like abandonment to let go of the terror in our hearts in exchange for the hope God offers.

Sometimes, something inside our heart tells us to give up on hope and continue to live in our sorrow.

But I don't think Jeremiah gave up his lamentations when he turned his heart over to God's love and faithfulness. God didn't wipe away the remembrance of people who turned against Him, nor did He erase the thoughts Jeremiah had of the times he felt that God had rejected him. No, the reality of the lamentations is that even in the middle of our pain, our sorrow, our trouble, God works.

My heart will never let go of my daughter's memory for one second. I will never let her spirit of love and life be far from me. Yet through even those times when I tearfully recall her life and pine for what might have been, I can also carry with me the truths that Jeremiah found so helpful. I can live in the reality of God's love, look to the future with God's hope, start the day with God's faithfulness—and tell myself as Jeremiah told himself, "The Lord is my portion; therefore, I will wait for Him" (v. 24).

REFLECTION . . .

- What sadness are you hanging on to? What loss? Do you feel that there is room in your life for God's hope and your loss to co-exist?
- What does it actually mean to turn our hearts over to God's love and faithfulness? Contemplate that action. Think of how it can change your life to do that.

THE ONE AND ONLY

What's behind it . . .

I'm sure no one saw this happening—no one but me—but two young men demonstrated just the opposite of what the following devotional points out. While older adults in positions of leadership struggled to know how to help Steve in his displeasure with God for allowing his sister to be taken "early" (our word, not God's), two of his friends never left him or forsook him.

For several years, while Steve struggled—and until he righted his life and returned to the joy of his salvation—these high school classmates continued to love him, accept him, contact him, forgive him, understand him, and be Jesus for him.

I am so grateful that these teenagers-heading-into-adulthood refused to give up on their buddy as he tried to figure life out. They didn't have degrees in theology or letters after their names, but they had Jesus in their heart and love in their lives.

They loved. They advised. They waited. They prayed.

While others couldn't figure out what to do, they were "close to the brokenhearted," and they sought to save "the crushed in spirit."

But what if in your pain you don't have guys like Marcus and Andrew?

You have the Lord. You have the promise. You have hope.

GOD'S WORD ON IT . . .

The Lord is close to the brokenhearted and saves those who are crushed in spirit.

Psalm 34:18

SERIOUS CONTEMPLATION . . .

The promise of Psalm 34:18 is good news of the highest order. It is the kind of good news that gives hope in the face of one of the worst realities experienced by those who have suffered loss.

That reality is this: people, no matter how well-intentioned, will fail in their efforts to bring comfort to the comfortless. They will try. They will surely try. But they will stumble in their efforts from time to time.

When they fail us, how good it is to know that "the Lord is close to the brokenhearted."

Well-intentioned stumbles happened to us. Not often, but often enough.

While we were blessed with an encouraging multitude of comforters, there were times when the people we needed the most were simply not able to give the care we needed.

For instance, when we pleaded with those who had influence in our son's life to come alongside him as he groped through his darkest days without Melissa, our pleas often failed to bring results. Not always, but far too often.

When we needed spiritual leaders to walk with us or be with us or simply acknowledge us—they were often AWOL from the battle we faced. Not knowing how to handle a family that had an out-of-order death, many opted to stay on the sidelines.

This happens to everyone who walks through the valley. The road is long, and it is understandable that friends, clergy, teachers, relatives, and others have their own paths they must tread. Also, would-be comforters often either feel ill-equipped or are too invested in their own journey (rightly so) to come alongside the grieving or the suffering or the beleaguered.

Psalm 34:18 becomes great news when that happens.

It says that if we have hearts that are broken for whatever reason and if our spirit lies crushed beneath the weight of circumstances that are far too heavy for us to bear—Someone is there. Someone is at our shoulder on the valley road. Someone is there to hear our groaning, to hold our quivering hand, and to put balm on our damaged heart.

Listen: "The Lord is close to the brokenhearted and saves those who are crushed in spirit."

Let those words sink in. Store them away for a time of need. Savor the comfort of realizing that if humans fail us in their humanness, we have Someone who will put His arms of love around us and lift our spirits.

Whisper your sad thoughts to him, and He says, "I understand."

Cry out with your despair, and He says, "I've been there. I care."

Let the tears of your tragedy run down your cheeks and onto His shoulder, and He says, "Here, let me wipe those with my love and mercy."

Show Him your brokenness, and listen as He says, "I can heal that."

God has surrounded us with friends, loved ones, and others who do what they can to help us face the losses of life. But sometimes, those comforters with flesh on can't quite carry the load.

That's okay. God can. Feel His closeness. Experience His rescue.

Walk by the side of the only One who will never fail.

REFLECTION . . .

- Is someone letting you down in your hour of need? You do know that there is Someone who won't, don't you? Turn to Him.
- Is someone staying with you and being Jesus to you in your time of despair? Don't forget to say thanks. This friend may end up needing your comfort, help, and compassion someday.

CHAPTER
FIVE

FEARING NO EVIL

Walking down life's roads can lead to fear—a logical fear of the forces that oppose goodness and light. The most fearsome of those roads could well be the one that passes through the valley of the shadow of death. But even in those worst of times a promise stands clear—a promise that can get us beyond the valley. It is the promise that even on that road, "I will fear no evil."

LIKE A DEATH

What's behind it . . .

When I returned to the office at RBC Ministries after Melissa's death, it was difficult to get any work done for quite a few days. Of course, one reason was that my mind was not really on trying to get interviews with athletes or planning a sports magazine. It all seemed so inconsequential and silly. Even baseball seemed like a waste of my time.

But another reason work was secondary for a while was that I had a continual parade of co-workers stopping by my office.

One was a man who shared an insight with me that I have not forgotten. He took the chance to compare my grief with a different kind of grief that he had suffered. That is taking a chance—because as has been noted, comparison of troubles sometimes seems inappropriate.

This, surprisingly, wasn't.

Many years earlier, his wife had surprised him with the announcement that she wanted a divorce. My friend, a Christian leader, had no idea it was coming—and he had done nothing that he knew of to cause it.

He shared with me that his divorce was like a death. He had grieved the dissolution of his marriage. And though he had successfully and biblically remarried, he continued to feel that pain.

GOD'S WORD ON IT . . .

A man will leave his father and mother and be united to his wife, and they will become one flesh.

Genesis 2:24

SERIOUS CONTEMPLATION . . .

Two people. Joined as one. One flesh. United.

What a picture. Marriage at its best welds two people as nothing else can do. It is a leaving behind of one unit—

the parent-child relationship—and the moving into another kind of unit—one that at its finest is inseparable.

When it works, it is beautiful. It is godly. It is a grand mystery with a marvelous ending.

That is what makes the dissolution of a marriage so ugly.

Two people. Now ripped apart. One flesh divided. Un-united.

No wonder it is such a loss for those who strive to live as God commanded us to live. What began as a faithful leap toward hope and happiness has become an unraveled tapestry of pain. Threads rip. A masterpiece lies in disarray. What once was a glorious picture of love has become a shredded canvas of shattered dreams.

What hope can come from this loss? What steps in God's direction can encourage those, who like my colleague, saw divorce as something very much like a death?

It begins where marriage began: love.

While it appears in a divorce that love failed, the one who feels deserted by love can find an unfailing, limitless, never-ending love to help rebuild a life. Psalm 147:11 reminds us that even though humans may let us down, we can put our hope in God's "unfailing love."

When a child of God suffers through divorce and all it does to bring pain, another thing he or she needs is renewed strength. Just like grief, divorce saps the energy out of those who are enduring it. It may seem that hope died with the signing of the papers, but it can be renewed. When it is directed toward God and His unfailing love, here's what happens: "Those who hope in the Lord will renew their strength" (Isaiah 40:31).

The excitement of a new marriage suggests youthfulness and vigor. So does the next part of the verse: "They will soar on wings like eagles; they will run and not grow weary [remember the weariness of a disintegrating marriage], they will walk and not faint."

A marriage that you thought was permanent but that turned out to be temporary can also make you long for something of lasting value. Titus 1:2 can remind you of something you have that will never end: "a faith and knowledge resting on the hope of eternal life."

Unfailing love.

The ability to soar again.

Eternal hope.

Three things that divorce cannot take away from you. Three things that can restore your feeling that life is still worthwhile. Three things that remind you that God will never leave you nor forsake you.

Divorce is like a death. But glimmers of hope can shine through this tragic loss as you turn toward the One who is love personified.

REFLECTION . . .

- If you have suffered through divorce, how is it like a death for you? What part of the knowledge of God's love has helped you the most?
- As with the death of a loved one, in a divorce other questions arise, such as "Why me?" "How could this happen?" "Why didn't God stop it when I prayed?"

Look again at some of the devotionals (especially in chapter 1) that deal with God's sovereignty in our lives and in responding to prayer. How can these articles help you if you are grieving a divorce?

BLESSINGS AND DISABILITIES

What's behind it . . .

During a mission trip to Jamaica, one of the most poignant stops the group of high school students I was travelling with made was at West Haven, a home for mentally and physically handicapped children and teenagers.

Among the youngsters our kids played with, fed, and ministered to during our stay were some boys and girls who were profoundly impaired. Their existence consisted solely of being in a wheelchair—with a complete inability to interact, speak, communicate, see, or hear.

What an eye-opener this was for our teenagers!

Our teens had to think through what it means for a child to live in a way that was so foreign to them—so unable to do anything. How could they process the pain and the hopelessness that they were seeing?

The loss of the ability to live in a body that is not whole has been well documented by such spiritual giants as Joni Eareckson Tada. We learn so much about others when we consider God's role in the midst of physical disability.

Whether we deal with people like these directly—as those American teens did or as my wife does as she cares for

profoundly handicapped children as a private duty nurse—
we must consider this loss and how we should respond.

GOD'S WORD ON IT . . .

*But when you give a banquet, invite the poor, the crip-
pled, the lame, the blind, and you will be blessed.*
Luke 14:13–14a

SERIOUS CONTEMPLATION . . .

The little girl cannot see, cannot hear. Her multiple illnesses
make her vulnerable to infection and illness. Unable to tend
to her own body, she must have continual nursing care.

In one sense, she cannot offer society anything of value.
She'll never draw a picture to put on the refrigerator. She'll
never kick a soccer ball, add up two numbers, text-message a
friend, see the sunset, or sing a Hannah Montana song.

Yet she is valuable beyond measure.

Her family adores her. Her sisters love to be with her,
climb into bed with her, push her wheelchair. Her mother
loves to make her look adorable for the school she attends
with other disabled kids. She dresses her up as a Disney
character for Halloween so she can go trick-or-treat. Her dad
dotes over her as any loving dad does.

This is a hard life for the whole family. It means addi-
tional costs. An expensive van. Special living arrangements.
Multiple hospital visits. The presence of nurses in the house.

But it is a life. A valuable, precious life.

A life that is different from those kids in that orphanage in Jamaica but valuable just the same.

A life that brings blessing to all who interact with this young girl.

After we visit that Jamaican orphanage so our teens can play with kids who have all manner of disabilities, they most often tell us at the end of ten days of ministering on the island in music, drama, and multiple other ways that their highlight was West Haven.

Look at that verse. Jesus didn't say that if folks show godly love for the "poor, the crippled, the lame, the blind" that the objects of their love will be blessed. No, He said to those helpers, "*you* will be blessed."

God, it appears, reserves special honor for those who see special needs and meet them with love and compassion. He expects us to be His hands and feet to give assistance to those who have lost what we think are the most valuable abilities—the abilities of a body to function properly.

But the most valuable ability, it seems, is to restore hope in the lives of people who might be hopeless without our assistance.

God's plan for all of His children—from the helpless to those who can provide help—is a miracle of His grace. To follow that plan gives the able-bodied blessings untold as a way of insuring that the not-so-able-bodied are never neglected.

We see the loss in the lives of the disabled, and instead of offering pity, we are called to come alongside to be their arms, eyes, and feet. And when we do, we both get one of God's greatest gifts: His blessing.

REFLECTION . . .

- Where do you encounter loss similar to that described above? In what ways can you help?
- Describe the blessings you've received from helping those who are not whole.

LOST BUT NOT GONE

What's behind it . . .

My mother enjoyed Melissa's funeral. That's because she didn't understand what was going on.

In fact, at the family gathering after the funeral, she looked around and said, "We ought to get together like this more often."

She was there, but her mind was on its way to oblivion. She was in advancing stages of dementia, and while she was still physically able to attend her granddaughter's memorial service, she was not mentally able to contemplate the gravity of it.

The irony of it all was that it was after my sister's death at age thirty-nine that my mom first showed signs of mental deterioration. It progressed for the next fifteen years or so until the final few years of her life when she no longer recognized my brother or me—or anyone else.

Her body simply outlived her mind.

That's another loss, and it's one that so many families must deal with as their parents live into their seventies, eighties, and nineties.

They are lost, but they are not gone.

GOD'S WORD ON IT . . .

Blessed is he who has regard for the weak.

Psalm 41:1

SERIOUS CONTEMPLATION . . .

She's there. Healthy. Eating. Sometimes even smiling. Talking.

But really, she's gone.

It happens with some of the best saints we know. They live well. They honor God with their lives. They serve and they love. They care for themselves well and for others better.

And then the light goes out before the party is over.

It's Alzheimer's. Or dementia. Two names with pretty much the same result.

It was dementia that stole my mother from my brother and me and from our families.

Our mom was a schoolteacher. Beloved in the community for her dedication to guiding elementary-aged kids through her wisdom and her love. A little tough-minded in her approach but a lot love-guided in her touch, Mother gave hundreds of youngsters a head start toward success.

We first began to notice the decline when my sister died. Melanoma took her and left her two teenage sons and her husband looking for direction. And it left my mother not quite the same.

She was forgetting things she never forgot. Occasionally she would even be a little irritated—an unusual trait for this even-tempered woman.

The light was fading, and at Melissa's funeral, it manifested itself in a most saddening way. While we sat at the church after Melissa's funeral, Mother looked around the room and said, "We ought to get together like this more often."

She could not grasp the fact that her granddaughter was gone. Later, when I would call her for our Sunday afternoon talks, which were becoming less intelligible as Mother moved farther away from reality, she would ask how everyone was doing—including Melissa. I would try again to explain to her that Melissa was dead, but I simply could not get through.

She was there. But she was gone.

Her last few years were spent in silence in a nursing home as the staff valiantly made each day comfortable, yet no day was different from the one before or after.

It's another *why* waiting to be asked, isn't it?

Why would God want Melissa's grandmother to remain on this earth when it would seem that to be with Jesus and Dad would have been more advantageous? Why did we have to watch her decline while at the same time suffering each day with not being able to see Melissa at all?

Somehow, it would seem, God is honored through this apparent reversal of logic. Mother's life still held value simply because God's action gave it value. She still received love from those who cared for her and from our family. Her life before had been valuable because of what she gave to others in the church, at school, at home. Her life later became valuable because of what she received from all who loved her, cared for her, and prayed for her.

The sovereign decision of God to take Melissa to heaven but to leave my mother behind is not ours to debate. Both Mell and Mom had impact and value according to God's design—not through our explanations or questions.

A series of verses in the Psalms comes to mind:

> *Blessed is he who has regard for the weak;*
> *the Lord delivers him in times of trouble.*
> *The Lord will protect him and preserve his life;*
> *he will bless him in the land . . .*
> *The Lord will sustain him on his sickbed*
> *and restore him from his bed of illness.*
>
> *Psalm 41:1–3*

As my mother lived out her life in the days and the ways God gave her, she was cared for by those who have "regard for the weak." She was a conduit of their care as they served their godly duties. Through her days of what appeared to be gathering darkness, God protected and preserved my mother, and her presence continued to remind all who knew her of the way she had been "blessed . . . in the land" as a respected Christian teacher. And finally, in a way that pleased us all, God finally restored her—taking her to heaven where in her glorified body she will forever worship her precious Jesus.

As we wait out the declining years of our loved ones, let's do God's work of caring for them, honoring them, and waiting in anticipation of the day God welcomes them home to His glory.

They may seem gone, but we should never forget them.

REFLECTION . . .

- How can we prepare ourselves for dealing with aging parents? There are financial considerations. There are living arrangement questions. There are faith-related questions. How can you be ready when this inevitability arises?
- Who do you know who needs care (perhaps not a family member)? How valuable is it to go to those who cannot return love for good deeds? How godly is it to give to those who cannot say thanks?

HELPING OR HELPLESS?

What's behind it . . .

People who have suffered a big loss have a choice to make, but it's a decision they usually don't make early in the grieving process. Believe me, it took my wife and me a long time to see our new life as grieving parents as an opportunity.

Helplessness permeated our life. We felt like failures as parents because we hadn't protected our daughter. I remember going through intense sadness because on the morning of Melissa's death I had not gone down to her room and talked to her (as was my normal practice) before she left for school.

We felt like outcasts from the normal world. Who else has lost a teenage daughter? Normality had left the room.

We felt estranged a bit from our life of faith—as mentioned before—because the God we trusted had allowed this.

I could go on, but you get the idea. Our new address was Helplessville.

Slowly, though, we found that there was a bit of a different approach that we could take—one that moved us to a new place in life: to the realm of the helping.

In your journey, see if this is something for you to consider.

GOD'S WORD ON IT . . .

I will say of the Lord, "He is my refuge and my fortress, my God, in whom I trust."

Psalm 91:2

SERIOUS CONTEMPLATION . . .

You have a choice to make. When life fires something your way that discourages you and causes you despair and defeat, the easy way out is to bury yourself under a blanket of self-pity and check out. After all, if life is going to treat you this way, it doesn't deserve your help, you might conclude.

You would be making the biggest mistake of your life.

Here's why. Because things have not gone your way, you have a unique and valuable ministry to others. You know so much now about pain and its effects that you are a ready-made support group for others who are suffering.

It's one thing to be convinced that an action is the right one; it's quite another to find a way to extract yourself from the trouble you are enduring and prop yourself up enough to take that action.

Actually, it's not possible to do this if all you do is "prop yourself up." It can only happen when we move out of the trap of our damaged existence and move into God's realm of safety. It will only happen when we, as did the psalmist, say of the Lord, "He is my refuge and my fortress, my God, in whom I trust" (Psalm 91:2).

Then we can move from the helpless to the helping.

Consider another psalm: Psalm 73. The writer was struggling with a question similar to the ones we who have loss ask. While we might look around and wonder, "Why do we, God's faithful, have to suffer trouble when others don't?" he was saying, "Why do we, God's faithful, not have the success of others?"

He struggled—he lived the helpless life—until He did a thing similar to what Psalm 91:2 says. He went into the sanctuary of God.

Refuge. Sanctuary. Either way, the act of entering God's presence and finding out how He wants us to react to our trouble is the final answer to the question: helpless or helping?

In God's sanctuary, in God's fortress, we gain the strength and the courage to become what God wants us to be: someone who takes the loss that has visited our life and turns it into an avenue of helping others.

The choice is yours. The choice is mine. Where will we go? What will we do?

REFLECTION . . .

- Think about the big loss in your life. Do you really think God allowed that in your life so you could be helpless?
- Where and how can you enter God's sanctuary and His fortress? What are the keys to getting in there and turning your life around for His glory?

THE ROAD AHEAD

What's behind it . . .

I have always been an optimist. Today was always going to be better than yesterday. I didn't quite subscribe to the adage of 1970s pro football star Joe Namath: "I can't wait till tomorrow because I get better looking every day." Yet I've always had good reasons to look ahead. Sometimes it was mundane reasons such as a baseball game I wanted to see. Sometimes it was more spiritual—such as an opportunity to worship on a Lord's Day. Sometimes it was just because life can be a lot of fun when you have stuff you like to do, a family you love to be with, and even a job that is right down your alley.

Even now, while always reserving a corner of my mind for the knowledge that tomorrow is another day in which I won't see my daughter, I like to get up and get going each new day.

Believe me, I know that not everyone feels that way. Not even everyone in my family shares my optimism. So it's a good idea to find help in God's Word for future shock—for the fear of tomorrow and what it might bring. Joshua just might be the kind of person who can help here, for surely as he looked down the road a bit, he had to have had some butterflies in his stomach. The road ahead did not look easy—no matter how optimistic he might have been.

GOD'S WORD ON IT . . .

Do not be terrified; do not be discouraged, for the Lord your God will be with you wherever you go.

Joshua 1:9

SERIOUS CONTEMPLATION . . .

You stand today at a crossroads.

Behind you is the past, full of its many joys and perhaps its frequent sadnesses. The baggage of yesterday rests at your side, full of both good times and bad. In a sense, you stand like Joshua of old—a man who had the wilderness behind him and the Promised Land ahead.

Sadness and excitement must have been intertwined in his thinking as he recalled the deaths the Israelites had experienced—all of the sorrow of burying those fellow wanderers who were not allowed to enjoy the bright future of the land that flowed with milk and honey.

And specifically, Joshua's heart must have been heavy with the pain of Moses' death. Moses was not a relative, but he was a mentor. He was a leader who had taken Joshua aside to train him for the difficult tasks that loomed on the other side of the Jordan.

Surely there were moments of happiness to be recalled as well, as over the years families welcomed new children and acquaintances were made. The blessings received under Moses' instruction and the reminders from the great leader about God's direction and love must also have brought encouragement to the people—encouragement that surely carried over for them as they stood on the precipice of a new experience, a new time.

In His love, God gives us those blessings. Even for the troubled and the heartbroken—for those of us who have buried children or parents—life is not all tears and darkness. Laughter can still ring out from our broken heart. Joy can still emanate from our pained soul.

But even that takes a bit of courage.

For Joshua, the courage to move forward resulted from a word from God—a direct, uplifting word that would send Joshua toward successful leadership. God told Joshua that no one could overthrow him, that he would expand the nation's holdings and that he could proceed with confidence because God himself would never leave him nor forsake him.

But Joshua had to keep his part of the bargain; namely, he was required to "be strong and courageous." And obey the law of Moses.

We face not a new land but a new tomorrow. Our baggage is not left over from a forty-year journey but from the sojourn of recent days past. That baggage may include a jar of tears, a pot of heartache, or a bowl of pain, but if we listen to God's words to Joshua—if we stand strong and courageous while clinging with a grip of faith to the hand of God, we can peer ahead at a new tomorrow with confidence and hope.

Our future can become a land of promise.

REFLECTION . . .

- What from my past have I not yet turned over to God to redeem and rescue?
- How can I renew my trust in God for a future in which I cannot possibly know what will happen?
- When do I need God's courage the most?

CHAPTER
SIX

YOU ARE WITH ME

The prospect of walking through the valley of the shadow of death is made more frightening if we think we have to tread that path alone. But God says we don't have to travel by ourselves. The psalmist's calming words are these: "for you are with me." God plus you equals an escape from fear.

NEVER ALONE

What's behind it . . .

I think the most alone I have ever been was when I was in one of the largest cities in the world.

Right after I graduated from college, I traveled with my college basketball team on an evangelism trip to Japan and the Philippines. Back in those days we took long trips, and we were scheduled to be gone for six delicious weeks of hoops and witnessing.

However, I had been hired for my first teaching job, so I couldn't quite stay the entire six weeks. I had to leave a week early to start orientation at my new job.

Therefore, I had to fly home from the Philippines alone. The big challenge was that when I arrived in Tokyo on the way back to the States, I would have to travel from the airport into downtown Tokyo to get my ticket (this was long before electronic tickets). Knowing no Japanese, I had to negotiate the transportation system, find the right office building, get my ticket, and get back to the airport.

Alone. I was surrounded by millions of people, but I was all by myself.

Ever been there? Alone in a crowd?

Alone at work?

Maybe even alone at church?

Alone in the quiet of your home relaxing after a tough day is one thing. Being alone while surrounded by people who you feel no connection with can be scary and intimidating.

Think about being alone.

And then read about what God can do for your aloneness.

Whether you are in Tokyo or Toledo, God can take it away.

GOD'S WORD ON IT . . .

O Lord, you have searched me
and you know me.
You know when I sit and when I rise;
you perceive my thoughts from afar.

Psalm 139:1–2

SERIOUS CONTEMPLATION . . .

An old song from the 1970s complained, "One is the loneli-est number that you'll ever do." Three Dog Night was right. Being alone—whether really truly by yourself or simply feeling that you are alone even in the middle of a crowded room—is not a good place to be.

We are made for companionship, so if we ever feel like it is "me against the world," anguish and despair can over-whelm us.

Sometimes that feeling of being alone comes when we think there is no one else in the world who can understand how we feel. This can happen even when you share an expe-rience with someone else, because no two people experience life exactly in unison.

Even husbands and wives who have struggled through the same seasons of trouble—whether it's a child who has gone astray, a financial reversal, or some other trial—some-times do not mirror each other's feelings.

While one of the partners might find outlets for help and hope in the midst of trials, the other could internalize the struggle, notice that the other is doing "okay," and conclude that not even his or her best friend is a kindred spirit in the situation at hand.

Psalm 139 offers a solution to such nagging feelings of being "the loneliest number." The solution revolves around a series of remarkable statements about our almighty God, the masterful creator and sustainer of all that exists, the majestic One who sits enthroned over all the universe and who has limitless power and knowledge. Those statements about God boil down to this:

God knows you.

Really, really knows you.

He knows you so well that when He is around (which He always is), you are forced to admit that you are not really alone.

After all, who else knows . . .

- whenever you sit or whenever you stand up?
- what your thoughts are?
- where you are going and when you are resting?
- what your plans are?
- what you are going to say before you say it?

He has to be paying attention to you to know this stuff.

And if He is paying attention so closely, you have to admit that you are never ever alone.

This could be spooky if it were anyone else. But because it is God, it is comforting. It is uplifting. It is a miracle of care, concern, and companionship.

When you feel afraid because you don't think anyone else quite understands the difficulty of your circumstance, remember this: God is with you, and He's full of knowledge about your situation.

When you feel left behind by people who don't have time to truly understand what you are encountering in life, remember this: God is next to you to remind you that He is there to comfort you (2 Corinthians 1:3–4).

When you think you have no resources to tackle the obstacle that lies in front of you, remember this: God is walking with you, offering His strong arm to help.

One would be the loneliest number that you could ever do—but you can't do one because God will never leave you nor forsake you. And He will lay His hand of protection on you (v. 5).

"Such knowledge is too wonderful for me" (v. 6). But it is true.

Hold onto it as your source of help in life's loneliest times.

REFLECTION . . .

- When do I most feel God's presence?
- When do I feel an estrangement between God and me?
- What are the three most prevalent ways God shows His closeness to me?

"HEY, GOD, IT'S ME!"

What's behind it . . .

On the night of Melissa's accident, before we learned that she had died, we got a phone call from one of her friends who told us that she thought Melissa might have been in a car accident. The optimist, I immediately assumed the accident was a fender bender. My wife, a realist, simply said, "Let's pray for Melissa."

We prayed. We didn't know she was already gone.

Praying for Melissa was nothing new. We often prayed for her protection. She was a young driver, so we prayed for her safety as she traveled.

We prayed for her spiritually. We prayed for her academically. We prayed for her athletically.

For all of our children, we prayed through their lives, their schooling, their friendships.

We prayed, but we lost Melissa.

It's another issue that I have to think a lot about. It can be troubling to consider that God heard us in our pleadings about her and decided to allow what He allowed.

Prayer is a mystery. I've tried to unfold one aspect of it that Melissa's death has led me to deal with the best I can. I hope it helps.

GOD'S WORD ON IT . . .

Three times I pleaded with the Lord to take [the thorn] away from me. But he said to me, "My grace is sufficient for you, for my power is made perfect in weakness."
2 Corinthians 12:8–9

SERIOUS CONTEMPLATION . . .

The mystery of unanswered prayer might not be so bad to deal with if it went something like this: You pray to God for five days because you want a new Mercedes. At the end of five days you don't get the Mercedes, so you conclude that God was either not listening or said no.

You might be a little disappointed that you still had to drive around in a rusty Plymouth Reliant, but you'd be okay. This wasn't like life or death or something.

The problem is that sometimes prayer is a matter of life or death. Or something.

And sometimes, no matter how hard we pray and no matter how much faith we have, God seems to be silent regarding our exceedingly important request. Sometimes we want to say, "Hey, God! It's me! Remember me? I prayed to you to trust Jesus when I was seven. I've been trusting you for the past couple of decades. Trying to do what you want me to do. Going to small group. Tithing. I'm even reading through the Bible."

But there's that family member who is sick. Has been for quite a while now. Godly person too. Just the kind of person you'd think an almighty God would want to keep around to do His work. But she's not getting any better.

You beg. You plead. You think a lot about the story in the Bible with the unjust judge who finally threw his hands up in the air and gave in to the widow because he had had just about enough of her knocking at his door. So you keep knocking on God's.

Yet she's not getting any better. In fact, people are starting to throw the world *terminal* around. Starting to talk about her life in terms of months left.

There's another New Testament passage that comes to mind. It has to do with Paul, who would seem to be just the kind of person you would think God would honor by answering his prayers. After all, Paul was beaten up for the gospel. Shipwrecked. Thrown into prison. He wrote books of the Bible. He started churches, confronted problems, preached the gospel. You'd think that if anybody had faith enough to get his prayers answered, it would be this guy from Tarsus.

So Paul prayed. And this wasn't really a difficult answer, it would seem. Not like curing cancer or making a quadriplegic walk again. Paul had what he termed, "a thorn in my flesh, a messenger of Satan." We don't know what this malady was or whether it was physical or spiritual—but we know that God doesn't have any difficulty defeating Satan when the time is right.

But God decided that something else should happen here. Instead of sending healing, He sent grace and power.

God's answers are given so that His will can be done, so that His purposes can be fulfilled. And in this case, it made more sense for an infinite God to display His mercy and His power through Paul's problem than to display His healing prowess.

See, when we pray, we must remind ourselves that we are not telling God what to do. We are telling Him that we have a need, and then we must turn the solution over to Him. And through His inexplicable ways, He does what will shine the most glory back on himself.

So as you pray today about whatever serious difficulty you face, or as you think back about something you prayed about and didn't seem to get the answer you thought was best or seemingly an answer at all, meditate about the responsibility God has in this. He is about making sure His story is told and His name is glorified. He hears. He answers. He cares. And the answer will reflect His glory.

REFLECTION . . .

- What is at the top of your list of things you have asked God to do but have not seen Him accomplish yet? Should you keep praying or give up?
- We can't possibly know what God is thinking, but try to imagine what might be some ways God can be honored even if your prayer is not answered.

ARE YOU LISTENING?

What's behind it . . .

I remember talking to my adult Sunday school class about God-doubts in the year or so before Melissa's death. I would always tell the class that I really didn't understand people who had doubts about God, salvation, and the Bible.

It had always been so plain to me. God was there. We prayed to Him. He heard our prayers. He answered yes sometimes. He answered no sometimes. He said to wait sometimes.

What was there to doubt?

I should have paid closer attention to David. He's the one who made it officially okay to ask God some tough questions. I knew that before Melissa died, but I guess I still felt that David should have been a little more spiritual.

How could he keep asking God why He was so far from him? How could he accuse God of forsaking him?

Finally, I got it.

I got what David was talking about.

God, how could you? God? God? Are you there? What have you done to my wife? My son? My girls? My life?

Are you listening?

When Melissa died, this David became that David sometimes.

I had to work through a whole new set of theological questions that I skated through before. The going got really tough, and I needed God.

Yet sometimes . . . well, sometimes quoting David's agony was as good as it was going to get.

David thought God forsook him. "My God, my God, why have you forsaken me?" he asked (Psalm 22:1).

Jesus quoted that question on the cross.

Who was I to think I wouldn't have to ask that same question?

GOD'S WORD ON IT . . .

My God, my God, why have you forsaken me?
  Why are you so far from saving me,
  so far from the words of my groaning?

Psalm 22:1

SERIOUS CONTEMPLATION . . .

Nobody wants to be separated from God in a time of need. Not the psalmist David. Not Jesus. Not us.

But when the going got really tough, David felt that God had abandoned him. When death was about to swallow Jesus on the cross, He cried out to a God who seemed far, far away.

And we must admit it. When we face our darkest days—when the joy of life has been ripped from us through tragedy or trouble or trial—we too can look up at the heavens and wonder why the God of all comfort seems to have turned His back on us.

Go with David as he takes that journey in Psalm 22. Join the psalmist as he cries out to a God who he feels has forsaken him.

"Why are you so far from saving me?" he cries out in despair.

Have you ever been there—in the far-away room with David wondering why God's hand of rescue can't seem to reach you?

"Why are you so far from my words of groaning?" asks David, feeling, it appears, that his words are not reaching God's ears. Perhaps he is feeling that his groaning is like that of a dying man in the desert—unheard and therefore ineffective.

David grows weary of it all. His cry fills the day and reaches far into the dark, silent night.

Yet David does not hurl insults at this hard-to-reach God. Instead he sends praises His way, rehearsing how God had helped his ancestors and how their trust in Him had been rewarded.

Keep listening to David, for now he looks inside himself and finds himself less than presentable—scorned, despised, and insulted. Yet David can go beyond that feeling of degradation. He can return his thoughts to the One who can save.

"Yet you brought me out of the womb; you made me trust in you even at my mother's breast. From birth I was cast upon you; from my mother's womb you have been my God" (v. 10).

The pattern is often the same for David as he works his way through the Psalms. Trouble. Despair. A feeling of rejection at the beginning. An "Are you listening?" complaint.

But then follows the good news. David experiences trust in God and hope in His hand of protection, love, and care.

We may feel like David from time to time, wondering where God might be that He doesn't hear our cries. But we must always, as David always did, return to the recollection of God's ongoing, constant care—of His ability to rescue us from despair.

God is listening. He cares. And He is waiting for us to come back to Him—to "trust in the Lord."

REFLECTION . . .

- When have I felt as David felt? When have I cried out to God in a dark, silent night?
- How valuable would it be for me to notice that David may have complained, but he always ended up clinging to God and trusting Him?

KEEP ON PRAYING

What's behind it . . .

Sometimes my grandchildren ask for things without saying "the magic word."

We all know what it is.

So Addie will say, "Can I have more ice cream?"

And my response is always to remind her to say please.

Now, is whether or not she gets ice cream dependent on her saying that word? No. I will give her more of the sweet stuff (within reason) simply because she asked.

Yet I keep teaching. I keep reminding her that there is an accepted convention in polite society: saying please.

I decide whether to give the ice cream based on factors other than that word, yet I continue to lobby for that word.

Although I love to hear Addie or Eliana say please, and I want them to learn to say it as a matter of course, I still can make decisions about what to give them or withhold from them without having to hear the word.

I wonder if prayer is a little like that—although the illustration is not a complete analogy. God wants to hear us pray. He has directed us to pray. He enjoys hearing from us. And we need to keep doing it so that we keep the lines open with Him.

But He stands in the decision-making position regarding what we ask for. We keep on praying because it's what He wants us to do—but we need to leave the answers up to Him.

Understanding prayer is a big issue in the life of all of us who have suffered loss. We need to think it through and establish a clear direction for this discipline of prayer.

GOD'S WORD ON IT . . .

Everyone who asks receives; he who seeks finds; and to him who knocks, the door will be opened.

Luke 11:10

SERIOUS CONTEMPLATION . . .

Who would have blamed me if I had stopped praying?

After all, I know that I had prayers—prayers about my daughter—that weren't answered the way Luke 11:10 tells us it's supposed to happen.

My wife and I prayed for all four of our children to be protected from harm and danger. Sometimes we prayed about it together. Sometimes silently.

But it was a diligent, continual effort on behalf of Lisa, Julie, Melissa, and Steve. "Lord, give them good health. Have them fall in love with you and trust you. Give them success. Find them good friends.

"Protect them."

If you have kids or have heard about parents and teenagers, you know that this kind of praying takes on added urgency as those cute little elementary kids reach the teen years. And when they reach the on-their-own driving years—whew! The praying gets extra intense.

Indeed, we prayed to God on Melissa's behalf: "Lord, protect her from danger on the roads."

We asked. We sought. We asked for the door of safety to be opened to her.

This time, though, our impassioned prayers for safety were not answered in the way we desired. It makes a person wonder. Did God not realize how much this would hurt? Was He not able to help a couple of teens get home safely on that sunny June evening?

The questions come, and the answers don't always return. But the key question is not about God and what He did. It is about us and what we do now.

Do we now stop praying? Do we go through the rest of our lives on our own, not consulting the God of the universe? Do we turn our back on the opportunity to present our needs to God?

If we were to do that—if any of us would ever decide to shut God out of our lives because He allowed something to happen to us that ran contrary to what our finite minds think is better than what His infinite wisdom allows—our lives would darken into fruitlessness.

Prayer is even more important to one who has suffered greatly in life. God is still in control. He is still the sovereign Lord of our existence. He continues to want to hear from us. He continues to desire our trust.

We pray because we have faith, because we depend on the truth that God has our best eternal good in His heart. We pray because while we see a side of life that is marked by sadness, God sees life from an eternal perspective that He longs to show us.

We still sorrow. We still weep. We still wonder and ask questions of God. But we also keep praying, for life without a connection to God is worse than our most painful sadness.

REFLECTION . . .

- What makes me feel as if my praying is doing no good? When that happens, what should I do to extricate myself from the trap of those feelings?
- Even after trouble interrupted my life, when did I feel that God and I were on speaking terms—that He was listening to me?

CHAPTER
SEVEN

MY COMFORT

Problems invade our lives, and we look around for someone who can calm our anxious hearts. We look for someone with healing tools. And then we realize that God has in His hands the authority and the support needed (the rod and the staff of a shepherd) to put our hearts at ease. Suddenly we realize that we can rest in His arms and feel His comforting love.

INSEPARABLE LOVE

What's behind it . . .

Remember when you knew for sure you were in love?

It can change your demeanor, your attitude, and even the look on your face. I remember back when my wife and I were dating, and I had taken her to my home church in southern Ohio on one of those "visit-the-parents trips."

I'll never forget one of the ladies in the church commenting to me, "I've never seen you so happy." That's because I was in love with Sue, and when she was with me life was spectacular.

It's cool that we still feel that way four kids and several grandchildren later. I'm never happier than when we are just sitting around the house enjoying an evening together or out on the trail soaking up an eight-mile rollerblading excursion side by side.

We've been through a lot, Sue and I have.

We've had a lot of great times, and, of course, we've felt the sting of death several times—parents, sibling, niece, Melissa.

I'll never forget something I said to our second daughter Julie when she was just a little girl. She had heard about a family that was facing divorce, and she wanted to know if Mommy and Daddy would ever do that.

I knelt down next to Julie and said, "Mommy and Daddy are never getting a divorce. We will always love each other."

Nothing can separate us from our mutual love.

It's a tiny picture of the love Jesus has for us. It'll never, ever go away. Not in a million years.

That's a huge comfort when we face tough times, because we know we are never going to go through those difficulties without our Savior next to us.

That's some good news right there, and maybe reading about that inseparable love can give you some hope.

GOD'S WORD ON IT . . .

Who shall separate us from the love of Christ? Shall trouble or hardship or persecution or famine or nakedness or danger or sword?

Romans 8:35

SERIOUS CONTEMPLATION . . .

Where can we find inseparable love these days? Perhaps it is best exemplified on a human basis with those remarkable couples whose marital longevity is highlighted on the *Today* show or was celebrated by the late Paul Harvey. There we hear about couples who have overcome obstacles (who knows how many?) to remain married for sixty, sixty-five, or even seventy years. And anyone who has been married at all knows that in those multiple decades there were multiple challenges.

Yet the light of love never went out. These couples demonstrate inseparable love because they made a conscious decision not to let difficulties or differences plow paths of dissension between themselves.

Married or not, each of us has the privilege of enjoying an inseparable love that makes seventy years of marital bliss pale in comparison. As followers of Jesus Christ, we have the assurance that our Savior will hang in there with us no matter what. We have God's Word on it that no matter what the nature of our problem, nothing can slip even as much as a razor-sharp knife between us and Jesus Christ.

The biblical narrative doesn't just mention this insepa-rable love and leave us wondering about its completeness. Like an insurance policy that spells out how we are covered, Paul's explanation gives us a long list of items that cannot ever drive a wedge between Jesus and His child.

Can trouble do it? Thank God, no.

Can hardship break the bond? Thank God, no.

Can persecution cause Jesus to break up with us? Thank God, no.

Can famine be the bargain-breaker for a Jesus-follower relationship? Thank God, no.

Can nakedness separate Jesus and us? Thank God, no.

Can danger be the catalyst for a split-up? Thank God, no.

Can the sword carve a line of demarcation between Jesus and His loved one? Thank God, no.

How incredibly encouraging this is for us all, because none of us is exempt from at least one of these kinds of prob-lems and the difficulties that are related to them!

Mull over this fact: No form of suffering can cause Jesus not to love us. No level of trouble can make Him desert us.

But unbelievably, there is more!

Here's what else can't separate us from Jesus' love:

- death nor life (that covers it all)
- angels nor demons (nothing good, nothing bad)
- present nor the future (forever and forever)
- powers, height, depth (you cannot go away from Jesus' love)

- not anything else in creation (just in case something was missed)

Let it sink in. Let it envelope you in a love that surrounds with comfort your trembling soul. Let it wash over you in waves of joyful release from the numbing difficulties that can cloud life's days. Let it soak into your hardening heart in soothing notes of righteous song. Let it ring out in your life as an anthem of praise: nothing can separate us from the love of God that is in Christ Jesus our Lord. Now take a deep breath and meditate on what that means for you this day in a world that is far too confusing for us to figure out.

It's Jesus and you. Inseparable.

REFLECTION . . .

- What are five ways God shows His love for me? How has that been manifested in reality recently?
- What do I feel can separate me from the love of God? Whose fault are those things?

HAPPY? IS IT POSSIBLE?

What's behind it . . .

At the end of the song "At the Cross" is a line that I have sung my whole life without much objection. It always kind of made sense to me because it pretty much described my life.

> *At the cross, at the cross, where I first saw the light,*
> *And the burden of my heart rolled away—*
> *It was there by faith I received my sight,*
> *And now I am happy all the day.*

Sounded good.

After all, salvation, which happened because of the cross, took away the burden of sin—and shouldn't that make a person happy?

But add a bunch of troubles to life, and then what happens?

Finances.

Interpersonal relationships.

Physical stuff.

Death.

Who's happy now? So maybe the song's premise needs to be examined a little in the light of reality.

Happy? Is it possible?

I needed to stop and examine that question. Maybe it's a question you've batted around a bit as well. You may be surprised by the answer.

GOD'S WORD ON IT . . .

> *Blessed is he whose help is the God of Jacob,*
> *whose hope is in the Lord his God . . .*
> *the Lord lifts up those who are bowed down.*
> *Psalm 146:5, 8*

SERIOUS CONTEMPLATION . . .

The word *trouble* and the word *happy* don't seem to fit in the same sentence, do they? It isn't likely that we would describe those who face troubles, trials, and tribulations while traveling through life with a word that means "happy."

Yet that's another of the absolutely stunning aspects of the ways of God. He is the master of turning things on their ear and reversing things from the way they seem so clearly to be.

Psalm 146:5 describes the person who puts his or her hope in the Lord as someone who is *blessed*. This word simply means "happy." The person who rests all hope—all desire—all anticipation for the future squarely on the shoulders of God is blessed—is happy in the truest sense of the word.

When we think about how this works, we might conclude that, of course, hoping in God brings blessedness. After all, He brings us things like nice weather, a good job, a loving spouse, a successful church experience, and all kinds of other really positive stuff in life.

But the surprise comes when we keep reading Psalm 146. Those aren't the end results for the people who are blessed according to this passage. No, the psalm-writer here is talking about people who are suffering all kinds of troubles. Notice the list.

God upholds the cause of the oppressed—if they hope in Him.

God feeds the hungry—if they hope in Him.

God sets prisoners free—if they hope in Him.

God gives blind people sight—if they hope in Him.

God lifts up those who are bowed down—if they hope in Him.

The bowed down. God works in the lives of those who carry on their burdened shoulders a weight too heavy and shares the load.

The bowed down. He enters the troubled world of the broken-hearted and holds them up.

The bowed down. God comes underneath those crushed by dashed dreams and gently buoys them on the sea of sorrow.

The bowed down. God cradles the crying soul who can't seem to see past the immediate circumstance.

Blessed are these people. Blessed because they enjoy the smile of God's goodness and care.

What has stolen your happiness? What life problem has robbed you of the trust you once had in God and His ability to sustain you?

Return your hope to Him.

Reenergize your commitment to put yourself in His loving arms.

Then experience again the blessedness that comes when He lifts you up with his undying love.

REFLECTION . . .

- How difficult is it for you to consider the possibility that true happiness—true blessedness—comes from a relationship with your God instead of from the circumstances of your life?

- Can you think of a time when you were happy in the Psalm 146:5 sense of the word despite being "bowed down"?

RENEWAL

What's behind it . . .

One of the most devastating post-Melissa aspects of our lives was the struggle our son Steven faced. He turned from a fun-loving teen who played tennis and ran cross country into a young man who no longer cared about any of the things our family felt were most valuable.

We felt terrible as we watched him struggle in ways that always seemed to predict destruction.

Thankfully, through a number of circumstances, he was able to retrieve his life from sure defeat.

It seemed that he was slipping away, and we couldn't do anything.

I know my wife often felt that life was slipping away from her as the aftermath of Melissa's death caused so many things to change in our lives.

It is so easy to lose heart as life takes what we value.

We see it around us as the American economy teeters on the edge of destruction.

We saw it when terrorists ripped our security from us and led us on an unfamiliar path of having to protect the homeland.

In a sense, we all face a kind of wasting away as we head into the later years of life—unable to do the things that once came so easily.

But here's what's so invigorating: God's Word has help for even these situations.

Renewal is available. Hope is on the way. Paul to the rescue again.

GOD'S WORD ON IT . . .

Therefore we do not lose heart. Though outwardly we are wasting away, yet inwardly we are being renewed day by day. For our light and momentary troubles are achieving for us an eternal glory that far outweighs them all.

2 Corinthians 4:16–17

SERIOUS CONTEMPLATION . . .

Slipping away.

You can feel it happening. Circumstances gnaw away at you like a relentless hunger that can't be satisfied.

It can happen, for example, when the child you so lovingly and carefully nurtured with prayer and care becomes a stranger in your life, a person you hardly know and simply cannot communicate with. Any such life situations—and each of us can give this generality far too many specifics—can overwhelm your emotions and strip the gears of your coping mechanism.

When that happens, the joy you once radiated—that shining anticipation of a happy future that was your hope—dissipates into a fog of confusion.

And you find yourself slipping.

Slipping away from the God you love.

Slipping away from the Savior you trust.

Slipping away. "Wasting away" as Paul puts it.

In your own power and in your own strength, you see little hope. You've tried everything. You've talked to everyone. You've pleaded with everybody to pray.

Yet that situation worsens. That child walks further away.

Everything in you cries out for surrender. "Go ahead," your mind tells you. "Slip away. Run away."

Leave it all behind.

Outwardly, you are wasting away.

But there is one more direction to turn—one more voice to listen to. One more inspired bit of advice to heed.

It's Paul.

He's calling across the two-thousand-year gulf that separates his life from yours. As you hear his call, you realize that you are hearing the plea of a man who knew trouble, who knew pain. This is a man, you realize, who attracted difficulties like a flower draws bees.

You take one look at him with your mind's eye, and you see a man who is surely wasting away.

He's hard-pressed (2 Corinthians 4:8)

He's perplexed (v. 8).

He's persecuted (v. 9).

He's struck down (v. 9).

You've felt that. You've been there. You've done that. You know the pain, and you know how nearly impossible it is to stand on your feet one more day against the onslaught.

But you listen again to Paul, and you hear him say the unfathomable.

Beaten-up old Paul is saying, "We do not lose heart."

The pounded-down apostle is no purveyor of Polyanna-isms, though, for he recognizes that he, that you, that all of us in the line of fire "are wasting away" on the outside.

But then he breaks the good news to us.

This is not about the outside. This is about the heart—where truly dwells our being.

Inside, he says, "We are being renewed day by day."

And then the real kicker: All that bad stuff that is sliding down life's garbage chute and landing at our feet has a reward at the end. Paul says it like this: "For our light and momentary troubles are achieving for us an eternal glory that far outweighs them all."

There's a prize inside after all!

If we continue to allow God to work on our hearts—to renew us each day as we keep our focus on Him—then we have this ironic assurance that we will be rewarded for our faithfulness. And that reward will trump by far the trouble we endure.

That's some good news right there, because that helps us see that we really don't have to slip away.

Are you facing trouble on the outside? It hurts like the dickens, doesn't it? But on the inside, if we seek God's renewal each day, we'll find comfort from Him now and we'll be able to anticipate great things from Him on the other side.

REFLECTION . . .

- Seriously, what seems to be slipping away for you? What is not quite as you wanted it to be—and you can't seem to change it?
- Have you seen others who were "wasting away" but who found hope and help from God's promises? Would it be good to spend some time talking to them about how God restored them?

CONTINUE IN GOD'S LOVE

What's behind it . . .

This might sound a bit silly in the big scheme of things, but for a long time, I felt that the worst day of my life happened when I was in high school. And it was about basketball.

Baseball and basketball pretty much consumed me during those years. I had decided to concentrate on basketball as a player, and I had one goal in mind—to play in college. I practiced by the hour. Between my junior and senior years, I spent innumerable hours working on my shooting and ball-handling. We were going to have a state-title contending team, and I was eager to be in the middle of it. Some of my friends thought I might be a starter in my senior year.

But something terrible happened. My coach apparently didn't think too highly of my skills, and he cut me from the team.

Devastated is too mild a word to describe my feelings. Truly, I felt that my life was over. I had no reason to go on if I couldn't play ball. I refused to go to school the next day, and I really didn't see why I would continue at this educational institution if I couldn't play ball.

Of course, cooler heads prevailed, I re-dedicated myself to becoming an even better player, and I was able to play small college basketball as a walk-on. Even got to be captain in my junior year.

You also might have surmised that my opening statement no longer holds true. Worse things have happened. Including what seems to be the worst thing.

But the point is that we all have events in our lives that make us think life may as well be over. When we start to feel that way—for whatever reason—we need God's perspective on the matter.

GOD'S WORD ON IT . . .

Now glory be to God, who by His mighty power at work with us is able to do far more than we would ever dare to ask or even dream of—infinitely beyond our highest prayers, desires, thoughts, or hopes.

Ephesians 3:20 TLB

SERIOUS CONTEMPLATION . . .

It's not over.

Oh, life certainly appeared to have drawn to a close when the worst trouble you can imagine visited you by surprise one day. Something close to you, near to you, dear to you left this world on that day, making the thought of day following day following day far too depressing to even consider.

It was as if the searing pain of the loss had made it impossible to consider a future that would mean anything but more pain. More sighing. More blank stares into a meaningless future.

At that point in life, it seemed so fruitless to ask anything of God. It seemed impossible to dream. There was no resource for praying, for desiring, for thinking, for hoping.

Yet the miracle of God's power and glory in our lives is that His words of encouragement were there before we even needed them. Long before our darkest night, God instructed a man named Paul to write down a series of words that more than two thousand years later could shine a simple stream of light into that night—a light that if amplified by even the smallest suggestion of faith could begin to swallow the darkness in its illumination.

It is in the province of God—and only in His mysterious, wondrous province—that a human soul bereft of joy can ever begin to feel joy's uplifting presence again. That is one reason we shower glory on our almighty God, because no matter what unspeakable sorrow visits us, He has the "mighty power" at His disposal to "do far more than we would ever dare to ask." If we will return to Him in baby steps of faith, stumbling as we do over our sorrow, our sadness, and our heaviness of heart, He will surprise us with divine portions of help we thought were too much to ask for, too much to dream of.

God can, and will, pour out new kinds of blessings that our "highest prayers, desires, thoughts, or hopes" could never imagine finding residence in our lives again.

Go back to God. Restore in your thinking the reality of the "wide and long and high and deep" love of Christ (Ephesians 3:18). Recall again that Christ's love "surpasses knowledge" (v. 19). And since you know that God gives comfort (2 Corinthians 1:3–7) while bestowing on us His miracles of provision (Ephesians 3:20–21), never let the pain of your loss block out the love of your God.

Life is not over. It will continue to hurt, but it is also still powered by a God at work to do more than we could ever imagine for good in our lives.

REFLECTION . . .

- Even in my life that has been touched by sadness or pain, what blessings have I experienced from God's hands?
- Have I ever thought of writing down God's blessings—perhaps journaling for a month how His love has touched my heart and life?

EIGHT

GOODNESS AND MERCY FOLLOW

Difficult losses don't equate to goodness or mercy when they first invade our lives. They feel like something bad. Something unmerciful. Yet God can reverse the pattern. He and He alone can bring godly goodness and heavenly love back into our hurting lives—reminding us that these characteristics in this life will find perfection in the next.

NO PIONEERS

What's behind it . . .

At first, you think you're the only one.

Even though friends quickly surrounded us when Melissa died and stayed with us as long as we needed them, there was a certain estrangement from them.

They were on the other side. They had their daughters and sons. They had not crossed this raging river.

So, at first, it seems that you are plowing new ground.

Seven months after Melissa died, a former classmate of hers was killed in a car accident. As I talked to the family at the funeral, I made it clear who I was and that Sue and I were on their side of the river.

They have become friends, and Sue is able to minister God's grace into Jon's mother's life.

We knew then, and we know more and more now, that when trouble hits, we don't start a club, we join one.

The troubles we face are faced by so many others, and we can help those others by joining forces with them.

We're not pioneers, but fellow travelers.

GOD'S WORD ON IT . . .

It was good of you to share in my troubles.
                              Philippians 4:14

SERIOUS CONTEMPLATION . . .

None of us are pioneers in pursuing the spiritual dilemmas that accompany life's struggles.

Just what our heavenly Father's role is in the drama of life's difficulties is among the oldest questions humans have explored. Indeed, the questions we ask in our investigation of God's role are not too different from those asked by Job of old.

The great man of the East, who clearly trusted God and loved Him unconditionally, struggled mightily with his faith after tragedy slammed his world to the ground. Job needed time to sort out what He had known about God in his life before turmoil visited him. Only then could he compare that knowledge with what He discovered about God as he slouched through the despair of unspeakable sorrow. Job asked probing, deep questions of God, and He wondered about God's dealings.

Job, for instance, wondered why he had ever been born (3:11)—a question that shows how far despair can go to wipe out the gains of even the most successful life. He wondered why God, who had earlier blessed him beyond expectations, had allowed him to be surrounded by trouble (3:23). And Job—the one who was blameless, who feared God, who hated evil—found himself without peace and without rest, for he was buried in a turmoil not of his own making (3:26).

Yet notice this: Job's questions were not condemned as he worked his way through the process of dealing with his sadness. Indeed, he himself called his questions "honest words" (6:25). That is a hopeful phrase for each of us who has become acquainted with life's downturns.

To be sure, none of us would be wise to compare ourselves with Job. And to be honest, his tragedies trump ours because of their severity and intensity.

Still, in one aspect at least, there is similarity between Job's life and yours and mine. It is this: Job's desire to love God, serve Him, and live in obedience to His commands. That is not the exclusive desire of this patriarch. And just like Job, when tragedy struck, those of us living in the shadow of trials honestly sought to know what God wanted us to learn about Him through our pain.

Often when the news turns bad in our lives, we feel as if we are pioneers—that we alone are trudging this path of stale hopes and trampled dreams. We can feel isolated, like the first one to cross a frontier in search of unknown horizons. Yet we must realize that our difficulties don't make us pioneers—they make us fellow travelers with some of the greats of the faith.

We walk with Job as He searches for God's presence.

We come alongside Joseph as he seeks answers to problems not of his own making.

We stroll lockstep with Paul, who made it his goal to serve God with contentment even when his rewards were imprisonment, beatings, and abuse.

Our path is not new. And our guide is the same one finally chosen by Job thousands of years ago. Our God is with us to push us toward home.

REFLECTION . . .

- When you think of the difficulties that you are enduring, do you consider yourself a pioneer, or are you able to find help from others?
- Is there a sense in which you'd rather suffer alone? How does that line up with biblical teaching about fellowship?

CAN IT EVER BE WELL?

What's behind it . . .

After Melissa died, her friends decided to put together a video tribute to her using the hundreds of pictures of her and them smiling and acting like high school girls.

Because they were high school kids, we wanted to make sure the video they produced was appropriate for Melissa's funeral, so I asked to preview it ahead of time.

When we watched it, we were touched by how well the girls had done—tastefully presenting their lives together as friends. And we were touched by the music they chose.

They picked two songs to run behind the pictures. One was "In the Arms of the Angels" by Sarah McLachlan, a beautiful song that made us all think of Melissa's home-going.

The other song was "It Is Well with My Soul."

The problem with that song is that it is so popular. So many times we are in church or some other setting and the strains of "It is well . . ." begin. It is hard to make it through that song without tears.

It is a remarkable song, and it means so much to our family.

The circumstances of its creation add to the poignancy of its classic sound.

And the statement of faith, "It is well with my soul," never ceases to grab my heart and challenge me as I grapple with the big question it presents: Is it truly well with my soul?

GOD'S WORD ON IT . . .

Do not be anxious about anything, but in everything, by prayer and petition, with thanksgiving, present your requests to God. And the peace of God, which transcends all understanding, will guard your hearts and your minds in Christ Jesus.

Philippians 4:6–7

SERIOUS CONTEMPLATION . . .

When peace, like a river, attendeth my way,
When sorrows like sea billows roll—
Whatever my lot,
Thou hast taught me to say,
It is well, it is well with my soul.

Really?

Mr. Spafford, how can this be?

Your daughters—your four precious daughters—lost at sea as they made their way to England with their mother for a vacation.

And you, Horatio Spafford, while sailing to join your grieving wife in the British Isles, stood on deck of another ship near that spot where Maggie, Bessie, Annie, and Tanetta perished and wrote on letterhead from The Brevoort House a song that has buoyed the hearts of believers ever since.

You had received that telegram from Anna, which read so cryptically yet so clearly, "Saved alone." In your mind's eye, you saw the *Ville du Havre* go down, taking your little girls with it to their watery death. You continued reading the telegram, and your heart was gripped by that haunting question of Anna's, "What shall I do?"

So on board your ship, as you neared that sad reunion with Anna, you set down the ultimate striving for all future grievers: to have it be well with our soul.

But is it possible? Can it be well?

Maybe not completely—not until glory—but there is some help found in the words of Paul.

Things were not always well with Paul. He had trouble before he became a Christian; surely he was a miserable wretch as his hatred toward Jesus freaks caused him to breathe out "murderous threats against the Lord's disciples" (Acts 9:1) and take women and children of "the Way" to prisons in Jerusalem (v. 2).

But then that glorious heavenly flash blinded his already blind eyes and opened up for him the light of Jesus Christ. And still things did not go well—humanly speaking. Paul was kind of a Forrest Gump in reverse, it seemed—everything that could go wrong with him did. Even as he turned the world upside down for Jesus, his own world was flipped on its head with all manner of hardships.

How well can it be for a guy who is beaten with rods in Philippi and thrown into jail for casting demons out of a girl? How well is it for a man who preaches God's message and then has to be hustled out of places like Thessalonica and Ephesus lest the mob attacks him? How well can it be for a missionary who is arrested in Jerusalem and has to be rescued from the hoards by soldiers? How well can it be for a preacher when the opposition plots to kill him? How well can it be for a traveling evangelist to be shipwrecked on the Mediterranean Sea?

Shipwreck. That brings us back to Mr. Spafford.

He declared that it was well with his soul. He obviously knew the secret of that other victim of a watery mishap: Paul.

How can it be well? Listen to Paul. He explains the soul wellness plan in three parts: Rejoice. Pray with thanksgiving. Let God's peace guard your hearts.

Rejoice. Always. Then Paul says, "In case you didn't understand, let me say it again: 'Rejoice.' " Clearly, Paul is saying to fellow sufferers that troubles don't eliminate the need to rejoice. This was no "Name good times, claim good times, then thank the Lord and pass the caviar" statement. This was a "When they are beating you and tossing you into a cold, stinking prison, rejoice" statement.

Step 1 to Peace—to having things well with your soul—is to acknowledge God's presence and His power no matter what the situation.

Pray. With thanksgiving. Paul gave us exhibit A on this part of the equation as he rotted in the Philippian jail. It was dark. It was the middle of the night. Paul was in maximum security with his feet in stocks. This would have been a good time to grumble a bit. Perhaps muse on about how he should have stuck to his old job. But instead, Paul was praying. He was singing. He was obviously practicing what he would later preach.

Step 2 to Peace—to having things well with your soul—is to forestall anxiety by talking to God, making requests and offering up sincere thanks. Even in a prison cell, there is something to thank God for, according to Paul.

Let God's peace guard your heart. The "peace of God" Paul called it. This is not like any peace the world offers. It's a peace that "passes all understanding." Does that not make sense when it is applied to Horatio Spafford and Saul, aka Paul? Neither should have peace, humanly speaking.

Both should have been marked by turmoil and torn with dismay. Yet they had what we cannot understand and cannot live successfully without: the peace of God.

Step 3 to Peace—to having things well with your soul— is to steer clear of man's explanations and rationalizations about circumstances and allow God's indescribable peace to envelop your heart in its protective reality.

When life isn't perfect. When trouble comes. Rejoice. Pray. Let God's peace rule. Let it be well with even your troubled soul.

REFLECTION . . .

- Sometimes, it feels that all is well with the soul. At others, the soul seems to be unraveling in confusion and sadness. Where is your soul right now? Feeling well? Feeling unraveled?
- Does thinking about the tragedy that befell Horatio Spafford bring you any kind of help? Perhaps a feeling of kinship? Or does it remind you even more of the seeming randomness of loss?

YOUNG DEATH

What's behind it . . .

It's funny how your perspective changes when you get older.

When I was a teenager, a friend of mine was killed by a tornado that hit her house. As I think back to that time, I don't recall thinking much about her parents and what it must have been like to lose a teenage daughter. I thought more about the loss in light of being her friend and about how it affected other kids my age. I remember feeling really bad for her sister too.

But I don't think it dawned on me to consider the effect the loss of a young person had on her mom and dad. I'm not sure if they are still alive, but I know now that if they are every day is another reminder of that tragedy that took place in the 1960s.

A young death affects many people because it is so out of order, because of what it robs from a family, and because it is life-changing for those left in the wake.

I now know more about this than I ever wanted to. I wish I had understood it those long years ago.

GOD'S WORD ON IT . . .

Precious in the sight of the Lord is the death of his saints.
                                                        Psalm 116:15

SERIOUS CONTEMPLATION . . .

Long before death visited our family, we were deeply affected by the story of a young couple we knew. Back when our children were young and we were still marveling in God's miraculous provision of them in our family, we watched at a bit of a distance as a young man and his wife suffered through the deaths of not one, not two, but three newborns.

Three times they waited out the anticipation of pregnancy only to be left eventually with a coffin, not a nursery. Three times a child was born. Three times a child died.

And finally, the babies stopped coming.

This couple's life, it turned out, would be lived with only lost dreams and shattered hopes of the terrible twos, preschool, elementary school grandparents' days, middle school trials, high school excitement, graduation, college, marriage, and grandparenthood.

It's the life of the unfulfilled dream.

I think too of another member of our family—my wife's sister, Mary. At about the same time the above couple was devastated by their unspeakable trio of losses, our family was reeling from the death of my sister-in-law's little girl. Even before Mindy was born into a life that would span hours, not weeks, we knew something was terribly wrong with her. Her survival was questionable.

Yet when Mindy died, the grief was unimaginable for our family. I'll never forget looking at that tiny casket and wondering why we have to make death provisions for little angels like Mindy.

A little while later, Melissa was born, and we celebrated her life. While Mindy's mom, Aunt Mary, slogged through each day wondering about the "what ifs" and the "what would be happening now" of a Mindy she hardly knew, we were able to enjoy Melissa and watch her grow and learn, laugh, and love.

Young death. It forces young parents into an existence of watching other little boys' and girls' life celebrations. Empty arms reach into the darkness. Empty hearts yearn for the tiny touch of those little hands. Empty ears strain to hear again that hearty cry of a child in need of Mom or Dad.

Those three little babies. Mindy. Melissa. And so many other little ones, middle ones, and teenage ones. Precious children of brokenhearted parents—parents robbed of growing-up experiences and the culmination of a lifetime of training.

But all wondering the same thing: Why was my child conceived only to be taken early—leaving me with a pain that cannot be healed, tears that cannot be stopped, a loneliness that cannot be assuaged?

Except for several important truths—except for one God-directed reality—this venture into grief would be a dark journey into hopelessness. And these are the truths: God is in control, He cares for grieving parents more than they can imagine, and He has a difficult yet vital, viable favor to ask.

No death, no matter how tragic and incomprehensible to us, falls outside of God's sovereign control. As the author of life and the superintendent of our days, He alone has the right over the number of those days.

No death is capricious or unremarkable in God's eyes. Each reminds us of His role as the God of all comfort, and each places on us a responsibility to transfer to others the comfort He provides us.

Grieving parents are asked, amidst their difficult circumstances, to become comforters-in-training—taking what they learned from the God of all comfort and using it to surround other sorrowing souls with a divine measure of care. Those who suffer young death simply have a longer time to receive God's care, a more extended training session, and an extended lifetime of helping others in need.

It's the job no one volunteers for and no one wants. Yet it is most noble. Because life is what it is and because God's plan calls for people to carry out some of the heavenly Father's most honored tasks, those who have lost children are equipped in God's school of comfort-giving to pass along their lessons to those who follow their trail of tears.

Young death is a terrible reality. But from that reality comes an empathy, a compassion, and a knowledge that is best used when directed toward helping others in distress.

Somehow, the death of a saint is blessed in God's eyes. Somehow, God comforts those who suffer that loss. And somehow, we who have walked the dark pathway of death must find it in our heart to light the way for those who follow.

This is why I write about Melissa—knowing that our story will be the experience of others, and God's hope will need to be conveyed. We learned from watching our young friends who lost three little ones. We learned from Mindy's parents. And now it's our turn to pass God's comfort along to others.

REFLECTION . . .

- Have you been around a family that lost a young child? Don't forget them. Send them cards. Send them e-mails. Especially remember the anniversary date of the death. Keep this in mind: They will never get over that loss. They move on, but they will never move past it.
- When you read reports about young death in the newspaper, make it a habit to pray for those families.

WHO'S YOUR TITUS?

What's behind it . . .

Cool story about the friend mentioned in the following devotional:

A few years ago, I was heading up a group of college kids who were going to Jamaica on a missions work project. When my friend found out about the trip, he said casually, "Hey, if you need another person, I'd be glad to go and help."

That was the last conversation we had about the trip—until about a month before we were to leave, and an open spot came available. I e-mailed my friend to tell him. His response told me a lot more about him. "I'd love to go. I already got a passport, just in case."

I was floored. What an incredible guy! He not only didn't forget his comment, but he took expensive action just on the outside chance we might need him.

We had a great time as we and a bunch of kids did some needed painting and fixing for some great ministries on the island of Jamaica.

We hardly ever see each other. But I know that Randy is one guy I can always depend on.

GOD'S WORD ON IT . . .

But God, who comforts the downcast, comforted us by the coming of Titus.

2 Corinthians 7:6

SERIOUS CONTEMPLATION . . .

Let me tell you about a man not named Titus. He was a friend—not a close friend, but a more-than-casual acquaintance. We talked from time to time about little things like baseball or our kids. Nothing deep. He was certainly not an accountability partner nor someone who went out to lunch with me for extended conversations. I felt that this friend and extended conversations probably never got together much.

But shortly after Melissa died—when the world was whirling with questions that had no answers and problems that would never find solutions—my friend walked up to me one day and without hesitation or embarrassment asked, "Dave, how are you doing financially? Is your money okay?"

That was a Titus question. That was a man who listened to God's call to extend comfort in a most dangerous way—by offering to help financially. My friend was comforting our family by saying, in effect, "If money is a problem during this tragic time in your lives, I'm willing to be a comforting voice of stability."

Think of how dangerous this question was for my friend.

What if I had said, "Well, we are drowning in debt. Sue can't work. The funeral was more expensive than we could imagine, and I just can't keep up."

What if I really had needed money?

My friend would have had to do something to back up his question. And I know he would have—whether by using his money or by soliciting help from our other friends.

I'll never forget my friend "Titus."

And he wasn't alone.

God doesn't show up in person anymore. He did that once with Jesus, and He's not doing that again until the trumpet sounds.

But God sends his team of Tituses into our lives.

It was a group of Tituses who showed up at our door shortly after we heard that Melissa was gone. Within minutes our living room was filled with friends who just wanted to be with us to do whatever we wanted.

At two o'clock in the morning, when my precious Melissa's body was all alone in the hospital after the accident and I decided that I couldn't stand not to be with her, my friends and a brother-in-law piled into cars to caravan me and two of my kids the thirty miles to see her and kiss her and say a gut-wrenching goodbye.

That night, it was Titus in the form of one of our church pastors who sat with me at our dining room table as I blubbered out, "What do we do now?" We faced three or four days of an unplanned unknown, but with this giving pastor sitting across from me, I knew we would somehow muddle through.

Troubled? Look for Titus. Surely God will send him your way—usually disguised as a friend, a relative, or someone in your church.

REFLECTION . . .

- Who can you depend on in life's troubling times? You may be surprised who your Titus will be.
- Can you be Titus to someone? Who needs you right now? What can you say or do to help?

CHAPTER NINE

FOREVER

Long days of pain and sorrow seem to have a forever feel to them. But each time we trust our God
in the midst of our pain, each time we let Him lead
us and guide us and take away our fear, we grow
closer to that day when all pain and sorrow will
finally cease. He helps us now as we endure, but
He also reminds us that soon the true forever of living
in His presence will arrive and we will live peace-
fully and perfectly in the house of the Lord.

GRIEVER'S THEOLOGY

What's behind it . . .

Don't you wish you knew more about heaven?

I sure do. And it has nothing to do with the little discus-
sions people have about whether there will be pets in heaven
or whether we'll play baseball or golf or whether there will

be a long line of people queued up at Moses' mansion to ask him questions.

No, I simply wish I knew stuff about the people I know who are there. Does my dad know Melissa, his granddaughter, up there? Is my mother thrilled to be healed of her dementia now? Is Jesus there as we think of Him on earth, or is He spirit? And, okay, I do want to know how much singing is going on.

Is there a kind of parallel existence going on as if the people in heaven were just on another continent and in a different time zone but are moving about their heavenly lives in twenty-four-day cycle as we do? Or is it so different that God didn't even try to explain the difference to us because we're too finite to understand it?

Without a lot of biblical documentation to go on, sometimes I try to guess at what things are like in our ultimate destination. Maybe that's just a sanctified imagination gone a bit haywire—but I don't think there's much harm in trying to visualize what Melissa and other loved ones are experiencing in the place Jesus is preparing for us.

GOD'S WORD ON IT . . .

I am going there to prepare a place for you.

John 14:2

SERIOUS CONTEMPLATION . . .

There is so much we don't know about heaven! It seems that it would be almost easier to write a book about the things we don't know about the celestial city rather than what we do know.

For those of us who have lost a loved one (death knocks hard on almost all doors, from elderly grandpas to preborn children)—and sadly that pretty much covers everyone—our minds reach into the realm of the unknown and the unknowable to try to decipher what that existence is like for our heaven-dwelling friends and family.

Because we who have an investment in God's abode think about it more often than those who have not yet been touched by death, we tend to come up with both questions and scenarios that may not occur to everyone. But what do we do with these thought-items that may or may not square with the orthodox teaching of straightforward biblical scholarship?

Surely we do not know everything about what the inhabitants of heaven are doing as they await the final consummation of God's great meta-narrative. We are given some hints as to what could be going on, but for the most part we are left in the dark about the realm of eternal light.

That leaves us, sometimes, to create a griever's theology of heaven—a collection of ideas about what we think might be happening with the ones we grieve.

For instance, there is the theology of the prayer message. I know I'm not alone in this, because others have told me they subscribe to this tenet of the griever's theology.

Here's how it works. We are told very specifically in Scripture that we have direct-line access to God through prayer. In reality, it would seem, when we bow down and send up our prayers, they arrive in real time at the throne of God. He should, our knowledge of prayer tells us, hear this prayer as soon as it leaves our lips.

Add to this knowledge the reality that our deceased loved one—who is absent from the body—is present with the Lord. That should mean, we hold in this theology, that if we are chatting with God and our loved one is in His presence, then He should be able to convey a message from us to our son, daughter, father, mother.

In my thinking, then, since my Melissa is "present with the Lord," when I ask God in prayer to tell Melissa hello from her dad, why wouldn't God hear that request and relay it to her?

Perhaps someone with a degree that trumps my MA in English can find the holes in my logic, but I am rather convinced—without doing damage to what I know about Scripture—that I can send messages to Melissa when I pray. Of course, it may not be until I am face to face with Jesus that I'll know for sure if I was right and if my notes got through to her, but for now this part of a griever's theology sure helps me.

Here's just one more example. Could it be possible that the songs we sing on earth are also known to the people in heaven? We know it happens the other way. We sing "Worthy is the lamb," which is clearly going to be a song of heaven. Of course, we don't know whose arrangement will be sung "when we all get to heaven." But if God has directed people on earth to pen such beautiful tunes as "Majesty," "I've Just Come to Praise the Lord," and "Amazing Grace" for us mere earthbound travelers, why would He need a different set of songs for heaven?

Therefore, in part 2 of my griever's theology, I like to think of my Melissa still singing the songs we sang together in our family pew at Calvary Baptist Church all those years. It's a great comfort to think that our family's love for great Christian music can be continuing as she gets a head start by starting to "Sing of His Love Forever" already in His presence.

Maybe you too have your versions of a griever's theology. As long as it does not violate scriptural teaching on heaven, I can't think it's a bad thing to speculate about what our loved ones may be doing as they bask in the light of God's love.

It is surely a better exercise for those who grieve than dwelling on negative thoughts regarding our loss. Scripture tells us that we do not grieve as those who have no hope, and perhaps contemplating heaven and what our loved ones are doing there is part of that more helpful grief that we share.

REFLECTION . . .

- Do you have a thought about heaven that helps you cope with your loved one's death? Does it correspond with biblical teaching?
- Why do you think God didn't give us more details about heaven? Do you think Jesus is still preparing for us, or are the preparations done?

I COULD SING, MAYBE

What's behind it . . .

Music has always been important in our family. Back in the day when cassette tapes were the big deal, we had hundreds of them. Most of them were Christian recordings.

I recall when we first got interested in what was the beginning stages of contemporary Christian music. Our two older girls were little, and Sandi Patty was just bursting on the scene with her majestic voice. We put her tapes on and filled the house with her songs that lifted our hearts toward worship.

Soon the kids themselves were involved. When our oldest, Lisa, was just three, she was singing solos for Uncle Charlie and the *Children's Bible Hour (CBH)*—a radio ministry that was heard all across the United States in those days. For ten years, she learned new songs week after week and recorded them for the program. All four of our children took piano lessons, and later Melissa herself joined *CBH*. She sang in a trio called the SAM trio, a name that came from the first initials of the singers— Senayit, Ashley, and Melissa.

Our radio was tuned in to the local Christian college station 24/7, and we went through a succession of favorite singers from Ray Boltz to Jeremy Camp.

We loved the worship time at church as we sang both choruses and hymns as a family—joining with the congregation.

Therefore music has become an emotional issue with us as well. So many times when we hear songs on the radio or in church, they bring us back to thoughts of standing with Melissa in worship or hearing her sing on the radio. Those memories can stop our singing and begin our weeping again.

Indeed, the loss of Melissa's voice in our family and our home is huge, and the subject of music makes me think often of her. Plus, it makes me think heavenly thoughts, for I love to think of her singing God's praise there.

We turn to music at important times in our lives, and it sometimes points us toward a marvelous future of song and praise.

GOD'S WORD ON IT . . .

I will sing of the mercies of the Lord forever.
Psalm 89:1 NKJV

SERIOUS CONTEMPLATION . . .

Songs touch the soul of the troubled heart. Even for a non-singer like me, numerous songs have evoked a mixture of emotions in the years since our family suffered life's deepest tragedy.

One that I remember reaching my heart was the popular worship song "I Could Sing of Your Love Forever." One day while I was driving to work, it began to play on the radio. It's an uplifting song, full of hope and worship. However, as its strains filled my car, I found myself in tears. I could barely drive as the tears clouded my vision.

But why this song?

I sat there in my car for a few minutes after I arrived at work, wiping my eyes and then trying to figure out why this song had affected me so. Was it because it was such an outlandish idea that someday I could actually sing? That did cross my mind (and would be good news for all who have heard me sing), but of course that was not my song lesson that day.

Instead, it was this: The song brought to mind a truth both sweet and bitter. It reminded me that while I was about to begin another day of normal work here on earth, my daughter Melissa was enjoying the privilege of fulfilling the promise of that song in heaven.

As I sat there knowing that mundane work awaited me at my desk, I pictured in my mind my daughter happily singing of God's love, directly aiming her voice at the Object of her affection. There she was—free of life's fetters and getting a jump on me in singing this forever song of praise. Mixed emotions surged through me as I got a glimpse of my little girl basking in the glow of God's presence.

Happiness for her. Sadness for me.

No, make that happy for her and hope for me. Someday, I will join Melissa, and together we will "sing of the mercies of the Lord forever." And when that happens, I won't embarrass her with my off-tune notes. Instead, our attention will be on the Sung-to, not the singer.

In life, joys and sorrows often intermingle, which makes the hopeful glimpses of a praise-filled future so heartening.

Amidst the sadnesses of life, I cling to God's mercies and the sure hope of the promised future, which make it possible to live with the pain of not hearing my daughter's voice anymore on this earth.

REFLECTION . . .

- How can the hope of heaven help me here to keep going when sadness still overwhelms?
- Who am I most looking forward to singing with in heaven?
- What song would I most like to stand on heaven's shores and sing to my God?

RACING TO HEAVEN

What's behind it . . .

The following "people" story about the painting *The Homecoming* is one of my favorites from our travels through the valley. It was such an odd series of events that would have me getting to talk to the mom of one of the teenagers depicted in the painting that I'm sure God had His hand in it. What was even more interesting in this whole thing is something I didn't reveal in the following devotional.

The mom I talked with when I went to purchase *The Homecoming* (you'll understand once you read it) had gotten in touch with me previously after reading one of my articles about Melissa in *Our Daily Bread*.

I have developed so many correspondence friendships this way. Dads who have lost multiple kids in accidents. Moms who have lost children who share my daughter's name. Parents who suffered the death of a child decades ago and still struggle with their loss. But rarely do I get the added bonus of meeting these friends in person.

By accident.

When I went to purchase the painting, the mom was walking out of the store. We made eye contact, but we didn't know each other. But as I began talking to the owner of the studio, I began to piece together the fact that the woman I had passed briefly was Emily's mom.

The studio owner knew that Emily's mom was working across the street, so I was able to walk over to her store, meet her, and have a long conversation about our girls.

God gives us these events, and it helps when it happens.

GOD'S WORD ON IT . . .

For he was looking forward to the city with foundations, whose architect and builder is God.

Hebrews 11:10

SERIOUS CONTEMPLATION . . .

The painting is called *The Homecoming,* and it was created by an artist who lives not far from our hometown. Just before Christmas one year, a friend gave me a print of that painting to take to my wife and told me about the little shop where she bought it.

I took the print home to my wife, and she fell in love with the painting, which depicts the artist's idea of what heaven could be like as loved ones who are already on the other side await the arrival of new residents of the celestial city. Sue was so enamored with the print that she asked me to go to the nearby town the next day to purchase a few of them for her friends who had also seen beloved children ushered into glory.

When I arrived at the small-town gallery, I got a bonus. In addition to meeting the artist, I met a woman with whom I had corresponded by e-mail. She and her husband, just like Sue and I, had lost their seventeen-year-old volleyball-playing daughter in a car accident. In addition to meeting Selena, I discovered something special about the painting that my wife liked so much.

The artist had used Emily, Selena's daughter, as a reference, and Em was in the painting. And in the painting, this beautiful young teen was racing toward heaven, depicted as a city.

Those of us who have lost teenagers remember with fondness how they lived their lives, full of excitement and with boundless energy. Emily and Melissa were always on the run—always going from one sports event to the next school event to the next church activity—barely stopping at home to let the car cool down while they scheduled their next adventure.

Who knew that in their rush they were running for heaven?

Who knew that in their hurry to live life with vigor, they were actually cramming as much in as possible because seventeen years isn't enough time to do everything a teen wants to accomplish?

Fortunately, Emily and Melissa were running toward heaven. Each had a solid faith in Jesus Christ, meaning that when their lives ended too prematurely for us, they were ready to step on shore and see Jesus welcoming them face to face.

The Homecoming is just a painting. But it is a reminder of the importance of making sure that no matter how hectic and active our lives are, the one thing that has to be true is that we are running toward heaven—that we have settled the sin problem by trusting Jesus and that our last breath on earth will be followed by our first breath in heaven.

Racing toward heaven. That's the direction Emily and Melissa were taking. That's the direction we all need to be taking.

REFLECTION . . .

- Are we so busy with life here and with the good things of life on earth that we fail to spend time contemplating what God has in store for us in heaven?
- What do I really think will get me into heaven? Do I think that in any way I can earn my way in, or am I convinced that Jesus' sacrifice and my faith in that sacrifice is the answer?
- What does the phrase "racing toward heaven" mean to me?

KEEP TELLING ME THAT!

What's behind it . . .

Imagine your reaction if you were to receive this note:

"I have kidnapped your daughter. Don't be alarmed, though, because she's in a lot better place than she was before. I've been able to provide a lot better house for her in a location that has better weather and the most beautiful setting on earth. She'll be well fed, and actually we have lots of activities for her—just the kinds of stuff she likes to do.

"She is perfectly safe, and no one is going to harm her in any way. You'll never see her again, but you'll get over it. And remember, she's in a better place."

You would respond with fury and anger. You would contact every authority you could reach. You would move heaven and earth to get your daughter back.

Your life, for the rest of your days or until you brought her home, would be consumed with rescuing her.

I feel a little like that any time someone indicates that my daughter is "in a better place." While Melissa's circumstances are, well, heavenly, I'd much rather have her with us, thank you very much.

Oh, I'm glad about heaven's glories, but to be honest, I'd much rather hear her pull her car into the garage, open the door with her usual "I'm home," and listen to her grouse because when she opens the refrigerator, "There's nothing here to eat."

Food's not a problem in heaven, I assume.

But around here it—and companionship—are pretty important.

So it's a learning curve for those of us who have lost a loved one to accept the fact that they get to experience perfection in heaven while we struggle with their absence down here.

I'm still trying to figure this all out and know what to do with it.

Maybe you are too. Maybe this devotional article can help us both.

GOD'S WORD ON IT . . .

We are confident, I say, and would prefer to be away from the body and at home with the Lord.

2 Corinthians 5:8

SERIOUS CONTEMPLATION . . .

Among the most bittersweet realities of the death of a loved one is this: that person has an advantage over us that is indescribable in its scope, yet we sometimes would like nothing more than to have him or her give up that advantage and return to be with us.

On two occasions in the New Testament, Paul clearly paints for us a picture of what happens immediately when a believer in Jesus dies. In 2 Corinthians 5:8, he described that event as being "away from the body and at home with the

Lord." And in Philippians 1:23, he says, "I am torn between the two: I desire to depart and be with Christ, which is better by far; but it is more necessary for you that I remain in the body."

For the bereaved, there is immediate and warm consolation to read these words and to realize that when the saved person we loved so much and whose presence we cherished with every ounce of our energy was taken in God's sovereign time from his or her earthly body, that person went directly to experience some kind of closeness to our Savior.

That's why when someone does take the bereaved person aside and reminds him or her, "Your loved one is in Jesus' arms," the sorrowing one's heart can feel a sense of comfort and joy.

This is doubly true, it seems, for parents who have lost children or young people to death. Our job—our primary function—as parents is to provide for our children a comforting, nurturing haven. We are always more at ease when we know our children are safely ensconced in their rooms at night.

But when we lose a child, we lose that control. We lose that sense that we can wrap our arms around them and protect them. They are out of our reach—seemingly out of the reach of anyone we can call on to surround them with love.

Yet when Paul reminds us that their absence from us results in a presence with our Savior, our heart leaps a little with hope. We know that now when we talk to God in prayer, we can ask Him to take a little extra special care of our child. We can ask Him to say hello for us. We can ask Him to be the loving arms we can no longer provide.

The distance will always be there—until we are away from this body and in Jesus' presence. But the thought of our loved one being in His company now can bring a ray of sunshine into an otherwise dark night.

As we travel through the valley of the shadow of death, we want so badly to reach the other side—to go beyond the valley to a place of solace and hope. Knowing that our loved ones live in the presence of our loving Savior puts us in that safe place, that reassuring abode of those whose true hope is in God.

REFLECTION . . .

- What is the worst feeling that courses through my heart as I think about my loved one who has died? How does the thought of his or her being in God's presence help me?
- If I had a chance to leave a message with God to deliver to my loved one, what would I say?

TENT DWELLERS

What's behind it . . .

Heaven is getting crowded, it seems. Crowded with too many people I know.

My sister—who died at age thirty-nine.

My dad—who got to live eighty-three years and make a difference to a lot of people.

My mother. My niece.

My wife's parents.

My daughter.

And dozens of others I have known or have known about.

These people all gave up their tents around these parts in exchange for a big old room Jesus prepared for them in His Big House.

And the more we see our loved ones depart this world, the more we wish we knew the ins and outs of heaven. We can read what the Bible says, and we can read books by Randy Alcorn and Joni Eareckson Tada, but we really don't know what we want to know about God's abode.

For now, then, we have the dual responsibility of making the most of what God has given us in this life—an abundant life, the indwelling Holy Spirit, jobs to do, good works to manifest, and a message to take to the world.

That's a big chore for tent dwellers, but maybe that's one reason God wants us to be so busy here—so we won't spend too much time trying to figure out the mysteries of heaven.

Heaven is an encouragement to us because of who is there and what is being built for us. John 14 and 2 Corinthians 5 remind us of that.

Tent now. Heaven later. Live in one while eagerly awaiting the other. That's what tent dwellers do.

GOD'S WORD ON IT . . .

Now we know that if the earthly tent we live in is destroyed, we have a building from God, an eternal house in heaven, not built by human hands.

2 Corinthians 5:1

SERIOUS CONTEMPLATION . . .

How do you like your tent?

In 2 Corinthians 5, the apostle Paul has some news for us about our lives, and it is that we are just camping out here. In fact, the tent we live in while we're on this camping trip called life isn't much to brag about.

The picture he paints here is of a person who knows that he's hanging out in a crummy tent just waiting for his mansion to become available. And while we live in the tent, we groan a little because it's nothing like what we will have someday. It seems that for the most part, the older a person gets, the more groaning against the tent takes place.

This tent image provided by Paul can be a huge encouragement to you if you have lost a loved one close to you and you know that this person had trusted Jesus Christ.

While we are saddened and distraught because we miss this loved one so much, there is some joy in knowing that our precious son, daughter, dad, or mom is enjoying something we cannot even begin to fathom.

An eternal house in heaven, not built by human hands.

This is no tent city!

There is within us a longing (it appears from reading these words of Paul) for that place Jesus has gone ahead to prepare for us. Paul said, "For while we are in this tent, we groan and are burdened, because we do not wish to be unclothed but to be clothed with our heavenly dwelling" (v. 4).

Heaven is indeed a mysterious place to us who are bound by mortality. Yet we know that our precious ones who have preceded us into God's presence have something wonderfully marvelous that we cannot have: a feeling of completion. It is, in effect, real life—a life we cannot know. Paul wrote, "that what is mortal may be swallowed up by life" (v. 4).

Life. Isn't it ironic? We think of our "gone ahead of us" loved ones as having suffered death. But instead, in God's way of looking at things, they are the ones who understand life—life with Him, life eternal, life immortal.

We love our tents. We enjoy the life God has provided for us in our tent city. And we have the added accessory, if you will, of the Holy Spirit with us to guide us and to guarantee our reservations in the immortal land above. As long as God leaves us here, we have the double confidence of knowing He has a purpose for us, and He has provided a great place for those who have left their tents behind.

REFLECTION . . .

- What am I looking forward to the most when I throw off this tent and get my heavenly dwelling?
- How do I sometimes lose track of the fact that what I have here on earth is just a shadow of what I will experience in heaven?

NOTE TO THE READER

The publisher invites you to share your response to the message of this book by writing Discovery House Publishers, Box 3566, Grand Rapids, MI 49501, USA. For information about other Discovery House books, music, or videos, contact us at the same address or call 1-800-653-8333. Find us on the Internet at http://www.dhp.org/ or send e-mail to books@dhp.org.